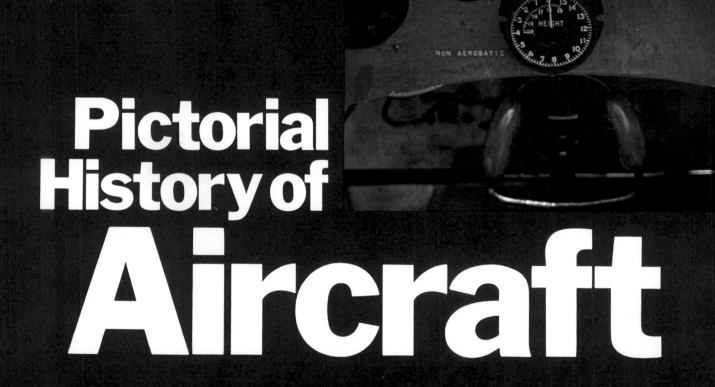

Pictorial
History of
Aircraft

Pictorial History of
Aircraft
David Mondey

Sundial

First published 1975 by
Sundial Books Limited
59 Grosvenor Street, London W1

ISBN 0 904230 11 2

Produced by Mandarin Publishers Ltd,
Hong Kong

Contents

Introduction

The 31st day of December, 1899, was certainly no ordinary day. It was, of course, the final day of the old year; but it was also the last day of the century; the last of the exciting stepping stones that were leading to what must, inevitably, be a breathtaking 20th century.

It could hardly be otherwise, for there had been such great technological progress during the preceding hundred years that the mind could hardly encompass the scope of man's achievements. Of these, some of the most spectacular had been in the fields of transport and communications.

On land, horse-drawn traffic had begun to face the challenge of steam coaches and traction engines and, in the latter half of the century, the first steam- or electric-powered horseless carriages were introduced—the first private motor cars. Then, in the last two decades, the first internal combustion engines had emerged in Germany: the earliest of them were powered by coal gas, later examples used petroleum as fuel. Though requiring extensive development, they represented a compact power source that was to revolutionize transport history.

It was also the century of the railway, with almost unbelievable expansion following upon the first steam locomotives built by the Cornish engineer, Richard Trevithick in 1804. Robert Stephenson gave practicality to the railway engine, and in 1825 the world's first public railway was operated by locomotives of his design and construction. By the end of the century lines of steel crisscrossed most of Britain, and London had even acquired its first underground 'tube' railway. By then, railway systems were in operation in most of the developing countries, the majority of them based upon the lead given by British engineers.

Simultaneously with the expansion of road and rail transport had come an extension of the world's canal systems; and with a growing ability to cope with large-scale civil engineering undertakings, some of the world's most spectacular artificial waterways had been created. These included the Suez, Corinth, Kiel, North Sea and Manchester Ship canals: the Panama Canal had been started, but was not completed within the 19th century.

Steam power had first been introduced to the shipbuilding industry in the closing years of the 18th century; but major developments came in the 19th, including the introduction of iron-built ships and the invention of the marine steam turbine by Charles (later Sir Charles) Parsons. The creation of triple-expansion high-pressure steam engines, that were capable of developing around 30,000 horsepower, made it possible to build and put into service passenger liners of up to 13,000 tons displacement. Able to maintain speeds in excess of 20 knots (37 km/h), these vessels changed completely the standards of inter-continental travel, signalling the birth of many of the world's great shipping companies.

Then, as now, regular, safe and fast crossings of the North Atlantic were considered a prestige-earning achievement: at the close of the century the Blue Ribbon for this route was held by North German Lloyd, whose liner **Kaiser Wilhelm der Grosse** had recorded an average speed of 22·35 knots (41·4 km/h) between the new world and the old.

Man had discovered also that he could survive beneath the surface of the sea—with a certain amount of compromise. The first successful underwater vessels—submarines—had been developed and, in addition, invention of the diving suit had made it possible for individual men to work under water at moderate depths.

There seemed no limit to the wonders that engineers and scientists had created. The phonograph—or gramophone—could play recordings of voices and music; the camera was beginning to suggest that it would, one day, displace the portrait painter; gas and electricity began to light streets and homes; telephones made it possible for people to converse over quite long distances; typewriters were in general use in offices; electric trams provided public transport in many towns; the first cinematograph theatres had been opened; and the electric telegraph allowed the rapid exchange of messages between towns and continents. Then, in the last year of the century, Marconi had demonstrated his 'wireless' telegraphic system, sending messages through the ether between Britain and France.

But despite such brilliant technological progress, there was a continuing area of failure. Man hadn't learned to fly like the birds.

True, he had found means of travelling through the air in lighter-than-air craft. Gas-filled balloons had followed very soon after the first recorded manned free flight, in a Montgolfier hot-air balloon on 21 November 1783, and many long-distance journeys had been achieved. But in no sense was this true free flight, like that of even a moulting and rain-soaked hedge sparrow, for the balloon was at the mercy of the wind and could not be used for transit between any two points at the will of its pilot.

The breeze-controlled wanderings of the spherical gas-balloon led to the belief that an elongated gas container, with control surfaces and some form of power plant, might be rather more manageable: this led to what was named the airship.

The first to demonstrate successfully the possibilities of such a craft was that built by Charles Renard and A. C. Krebs, in France. Named **La France**, it had a single large propeller driven by a 9 hp electric motor, and on its first flight, on 9 August 1884, covered a circular route of approximately 5 miles (8 km) and attained a maximum speed of 14·5 mph (23·3 km/h). It was, presumably, one of those days when even a kiwi's feather would have floated on the breeze.

This was to be followed, also in France, by the activities of the little Brazilian, Alberto Santos-Dumont. He had started by fitting a $3\frac{1}{2}$ hp petrol engine to a somewhat elementary non-rigid airship with which he made a number of flights in 1898. But it was with his No. 6 airship, powered by a 20 hp Buchet/Santos-Dumont water-cooled petrol-engine, that he made a controlled 30-minute flight, circling the Eiffel Tower in Paris.

The 'experts' considered there was a great future for the airship, and that it would be able to carry many passengers in comfort over intercontinental ranges. There had certainly been some convincing proof of reliability, for as early as 1910 Germany had a regular but unscheduled short-haul air transport service operating from Friedrichshafen. When this airship service terminated, at the outbreak of World War I, it had carried more than 34,000 passengers.

German development of these craft reached its zenith with the **Graf Zeppelin** which, among many other pioneering flights, had completed a round-the-world trip and several Atlantic crossings, before being scrapped at the outbreak of World War II, at which time it had flown well over a million miles.

But there were problems, even with successful vessels like the **Graf Zeppelin**. These passenger carrying airships were very big—the British R.101 of 1929 was 724 ft (220·68 m) in length—which meant they were difficult to house and maintain. In bad weather conditions they were a problem to handle, whether in the air or on the ground. Furthermore, the hydrogen gas which provided the lifting force was a potential hazard. When both the R.101 and Germany's new **Hindenberg** met disastrous ends, it signalled the disappearance of this type of aircraft from the aviation scene.

Even for military applications, when greater operating hazards have always been acceptable if the weapon in question offered a worthwhile advantage, it was demonstrated clearly during World War I that there were strict limitations to the use of the airship.

Germany built a total of 88 Zeppelin airships during that conflict, using them in reconnaissance and bombing roles. Apart from the difficulties imposed and the losses occasioned by operations in unsuitable weather conditions, their sheer bulk, slow speed and inability to make violent evasive manoeuvres meant that once suitable weapons were developed to make a telling attack upon them, their days would be numbered.

But with few other vehicles available to launch bombing attacks on British targets, the Germans continued resolutely with their planned utilization of the Zeppelins until 5 August 1918, when L70 was lost. Not only was this vessel the pride of the fleet, but among the crew who died was her Captain, Kapitan-leutnant Peter Strasser, the driving force behind the Zeppelin service. His death marked its end.

There were, of course, some unpowered heavier-than-air craft which had been flown before the end of the 19th century, but their flight was not that of the birds. Most significant were the gliders built by the German, Otto Lilienthal, with which he made thousands of flights. Even more importantly, he recorded carefully the details of each glider that he built, the changes made to improve it, and the results achieved, so that others might benefit from his work. He died on 10 August 1896, critically injured on the previous day when he lost control of one of his gliders and crashed.

Among those to be inspired by his work were Percy Pilcher in Britain, and Octave Chanute in America. The latter collected details of all the worthwhile achievements in aviation at that period, and published them in a book, **Progress in Flying Machines**. This, plus the enthusiasm of Chanute, had considerable influence on two of his countrymen, the brothers Orville and Wilbur Wright. For some time they had been interested in the achievement of powered flight, but it seems that Chanute must have been the catalyst which urged them to greater effort.

Technologically, the time was ripe. Success, for one or another of the many seekers after the magic of sustained flight, must have come within the first decade of the 20th century. But it was the Wright brothers who were to receive the well deserved accolade, the product of their conviction, dedication and application.

When early experiments showed that available data was faulty, they created their own, on scientific principles. They even designed and built a simple wind tunnel so that they could arrive at the most suitable wing section for their aircraft.

Early flights with their No. 3 glider, carried out over the sand dunes at Kitty Hawk, North Carolina, convinced them that they were progressing along the right lines, for with it they made many hundreds of flights under perfect control. Orville was to record that the flights which they made in 1902 ". . . demonstrated the efficiency of our system of control both for longitudinal and lateral stability. They also demonstrated that our tables of air pressure which we made in our wind tunnel would enable us to calculate in advance the performance of a machine.''

Not surprisingly, they returned home to Dayton, Ohio, with the conviction that the next year would bring attainment of their goal. The primary problem remaining was that which had been virtually insoluble until Daimler's invention of the petrol engine in 1885: the provision of a compact, lightweight power plant. By 1902 there were plenty of petrol engines being used to power motor cars and, consequently, the two brothers imagined that it would be an easy matter to acquire a suitable engine 'off the

shelf'. They were to discover that those available were far too heavy for, after all, weight had not been a critical factor for a road vehicle.

The only solution was to design and build their own, for they were not to be defeated at this advanced stage. The resulting four-cylinder water-cooled in-line engine developed about 12 hp for a gross weight of around 200 lb (91 kg). And when they had built it, they still required propellers to thrust the aircraft through the air. Once again, they had to use their own ideas and skill to devise the two hand-carved wooden pusher propellers. By late September of 1903 they were as ready as possible for the return to Kitty Hawk.

It was not until 14 December that they were ready for their first attempt. It was to end in failure for the **Flyer**, as the brothers had named their aircraft, climbed steeply after leaving its launching rail, stalled, and ploughed into the sand. It was a sad moment, for repairs were necessary and they were concerned that bad winter weather might set in before it was possible to achieve success. It was not until the morning of 17 December that they were ready for another try.

It was a bitterly cold day, the puddles rimmed with ice, the wind blowing between 22 and 27 mph (35 and 43 km/h). As it flattened the marram grass, scurrying the grains of dry sand, Orville settled at the controls. The engine was started and warmed up and then, at 10.35 am, the little machine began to move forward. After a run of about 40 feet (12 m) it became airborne and Orville, writing later, told that: ''The course of the flight up and down was exceedingly erratic. The control of the front rudder (elevator) was difficult. As a result, the machine would rise suddenly to about ten feet, and then as suddenly dart for the ground. A sudden dart when a little over 120 feet from the point at which it rose into the air ended the flight.''

Three more flights were made that day. The fourth, with Wilbur as pilot, lasted for 59 seconds and covered 852 feet (260 m), before a heavy landing fractured the elevator support frames and ended flying for the day.

As the two brothers, and the five local men who had watched the flights, stood discussing the exciting events, a gust of wind overturned the **Flyer**. A quick examination showed there to be so much additional damage that it was clear there would be no more flights that year.

Concern at the injury to their wonderful little aircraft was offset by the thought that now they had sufficient knowledge to build an even better model. Soon they would be able to fly again and, with growing experience, it really would be like that of the birds: purposeful, directional, controlled.

In the pages which follow we trace the story of heavier-than-air craft. There is no mention of balloons, airships and sailplanes, nor of spaceflight, for we are concerned with the main stream of powered flight within the earth's atmosphere. There is an emphasis on military aviation. This is rather inevitable, for once the 'flying machine' was taken to war it was developed continually in a constant effort to meet ever-more-demanding military requirements. In general, the improved standards of civil aviation resulted from developments which had arisen from attempts to satisfy the steadily rising standards of performance required by military usage.

The story of aviation is one of achievement, adventure and courage. It is written by men like the Wright brothers and those who followed them: the pioneers who sought to gain the freedom of the air. The realization of the achievement is difficult to express adequately in words. David Garnett in his book **A Rabbit in the Air** must have been very close when he wrote: ''For thousands of years we have crawled or run on the earth, or paddled across the seas, and all the while there has been this great ocean just over our heads in which at last we sail with joy.''

Powered Flight to 1919

Strangely enough, the achievement of the Wright brothers did not result in newspaper headlines around the world. This was due to a combination of factors. First and foremost, American news editors would not accept the exaggerated report received from a free-lance journalist. Conviction that they were correct in their scepticism came in May 1904 when, at a demonstration for the press, the Wrights were able to achieve nothing better than a 60 ft (18 m) glide.

This was particularly ironic when one knows that approximately 17 months later they recorded a non-stop flight of 24 miles (30 km). And even then the world was still unaware of the miracle of powered flight.

The awakening came on a cold October day in 1906, when a rather tentative flight was made from the Bois de Boulogne, in Paris, by Alberto Santos-Dumont in his No. 14 bis aircraft. Although he was airborne for just under 200 ft (61 m), this flight was witnessed by so many people that it was hailed as, and for some time regarded as, the world's first powered and controlled flight by a heavier-than-air craft.

Europe became the centre of the new art of flight and the biplane (1) built by A. and H. Dufaux of Geneva, Switzerland, typifies the aeroplane that had evolved in continental Europe by 1909–10.

In Britain, progress had not been so rapid. A. V. Roe was the first national to fly an all-British machine, on 13 July 1909. His mount was a frail-looking triplane of his own design, its wings covered with brown paper, the aim being to achieve an ultra-lightweight structure that could be powered by a 9 hp J.A.P. engine. Instead of acclaim for his achievement, Roe was threatened with prosecution for endangering public safety.

Twelve days later the Frenchman, Louis Blériot, completed successfully the first cross-Channel flight. He landed on North Fall Meadow, near Dover Castle, after an eventful 37 minute flight from Les Baraques, near Calais. Britain's 'moat' was no longer an impregnable defence that could be policed by the Royal Navy. And in the light of this achievement, the case against Roe was quashed.

Among the first practical aircraft to equip the British Army was the Bristol Box-kite (2) of 1910, which gives an appreciation of the design lead then held by the more advanced French pioneers.

Looking rather more as we expect an aeroplane to appear, the Blériot XI Monoplane is the type of aircraft in which its creator had made that first historic Channel crossing. That illustrated (3) is a prized exhibit in the Swiss Transport Museum at Lucerne, Switzerland. Not only is it an original Blériot XI, but it is the aircraft which, together with its owner and eight other men, formed the nucleus of the Swiss Air Force in 1914.

Design and methods of construction were improving: the most urgent need was a more reliable and powerful power plant. This, too, was to come from France, where Laurent Seguin and his brother had been investigating the weaknesses of engines then in use. The majority had derived from the motor car industry, and had the disadvantage of being low-powered and heavy water-cooled engines.

Early radial engines were also low-powered, and because of their greater frontal area caused more drag than an in-line engine of similar power. More drag, slower speeds. And low forward speeds meant bad air cooling, an overheating engine which lost power, completing the vicious circle which spelled unreliability. Seguin's solution was the rotary engine, in which propeller, cylinders and crankcase turned en masse, the crankshaft being attached—indirectly—to the airframe. The flywheel inertia of this rotating mass brought smooth running and the cylinders, windmilling in the airstream, were prevented from overheating.

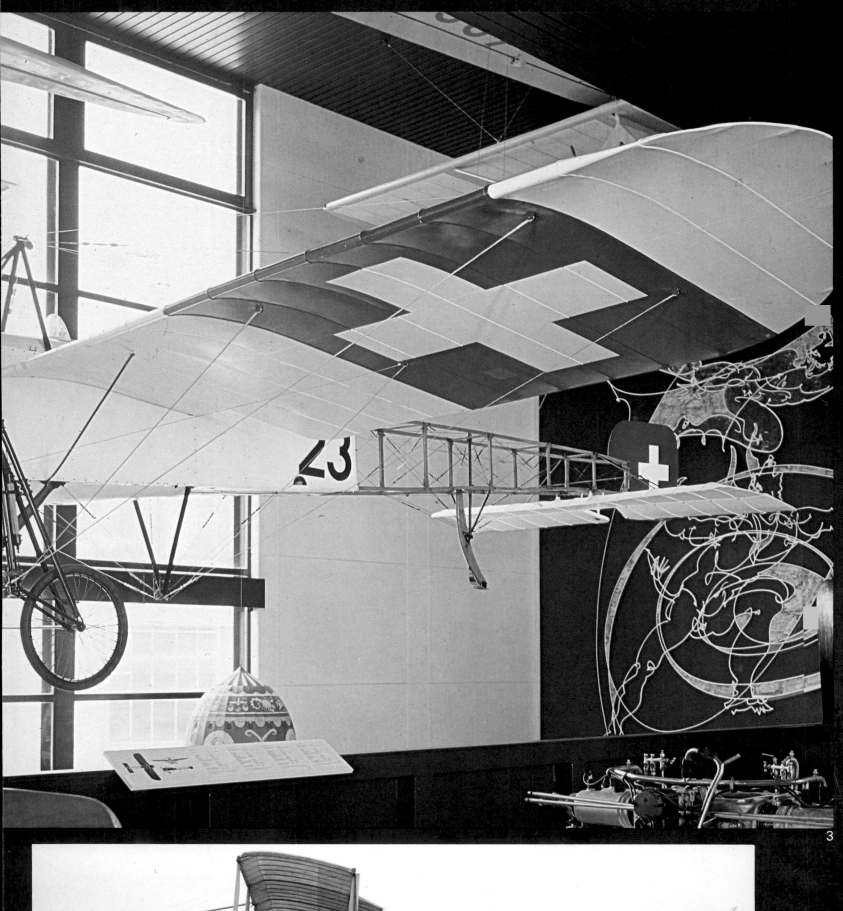

3

2

9

4

By the time that the aeroplane had attained reasonable reliability and controllability, World War I had started. As was to be expected, little time was lost in adapting this new vehicle for military use, although only a few far-sighted men could visualize it ever becoming a significant weapon. The majority of Army planners seemed to regard the aeroplane as an unnecessary complication to the art of war, delegating to it only the tasks of message carrying and reconnaissance.

It had not been appreciated in advance how vital was to be its contribution in the reconnaissance role. Soon it became necessary to use every means possible to prevent enemy aircraft from having unrestricted use of your airspace. So came the development of fighters to destroy hostile reconnaissance aircraft, or to escort ones own 'recce' machines: leading to bomber aircraft to destroy the bases from which they operated or the factories where they were built.

Typical of the more efficient fighter aircraft is this Hanriot HD1 (4). Note that it is of biplane configuration. Accidents with monoplane aircraft had suggested that a single wing was structurally unreliable, leading to widespread adoption of what was then the more robust biplane.

As the battle on the Western Front mounted in ferocity, so increased the demands on the combatant air forces. Early attempts to eliminate reconnaissance aircraft had been little more than knightly jousts, with opposing crews taking pot-shots at each other with revolvers or rifles.

But it was not long before aircraft were equipped with the far more lethal machine-gun. The main snag was that it could only be aimed properly and fired from a central mounting, which meant that the nearest target was your own propeller. Roland Garros, one of France's foremost pre-war sporting pilots, borrowed the

idea of fitting steel plates to the back of each propeller blade so that any bullet would be deflected before cutting its way through the wood.

He had considerable success with this device before a forced-landing behind enemy lines enabled the Germans to discover the secret of the forward-firing machine-gun. When ordered to copy the idea, Anthony Fokker devised instead an interrupter gear which 'timed' the bullets to miss the spinning propeller blades.

Typical of the more advanced fighter aircraft of 1917 is the French SPAD XIII **(5)**, of which many were flown also by the United States Air Service. That depicted carries the insignia of the US 94th Pursuit Squadron. Its 'Hat in Ring' symbolizes Uncle Sam's hat being thrown into the fighting ring.

Following page:
British designers and manufacturers had also worked hard to produce more effective aircraft. Army requirements had

been met by the Royal Aircraft Factory at Farnborough, Hampshire, where efforts had been concentrated initially on the evolution of an inherently stable aircraft. Ideal for unopposed reconnaissance sorties, it was at a great disadvantage when combat required evasive manoeuvres.

The British Admiralty had not been slow to appreciate that aircraft had much to offer to the Navy. This brought a variety of minds to bear, resulting in a wider range of types.

Among the Navy's suppliers was the Sopwith Aviation Company at Kingston upon Thames, Surrey, and typical of the company's excellent products was the Pup, with which the Royal Naval Air Service (RNAS) developed the concept of aircraft carriers. Shown on the ground and in the air **(6, 6A)**, so efficient were these aircraft—often rated as one of the finest flying machines ever built—they were soon to be adopted by the Royal Flying Corps (RFC).

6A

8

7

Bearing an unmistakable family likeness, but identifiable easily by its two-bay biplane wing, the later Sopwith Snipe (7) was another valuable addition to the Royal Air Force (RAF), which had been founded on 1 April 1918.

Designed around a new engine, the Bentley rotary, it was intended as an ultimate replacement for the superb Sopwith Camel, which had done so much to eliminate enemy air superiority. Unfortunately, it entered service in the closing stages of the war, too late to play a significant role.

But with the war's end, the Snipe became the RAF's standard fighter, some examples remaining in service until 1927. Snipes of No. 1 Squadron formed part of the original air control force in Iraq, a spectacular use of air power when the RAF was made responsible in 1922 for peace-keeping in that country, instead of traditional and far more costly to maintain ground forces.

Manoeuvrability was the primary requirement of those fighter aircraft involved in 'dog-fights', which developed on both sides of the Western Front as squadrons sought to prevent intrusion of their own airspace. This was completely the reverse of the inherently stable aircraft which Britain had tried so hard to perfect at the war's beginning.

Manoeuvrability required a compact and robust aeroplane of short wing span. But if the wing span was reduced too much, reducing also the wing area, then the amount of lift which it could develop was considerably less. This meant that manoeuvrability was gained only by increased take-off and landing speeds, a slower rate of climb and a lower operating height.

One solution to overcome these problems lay in the triplane wing, introduced initially on a fighter by the Sopwith Triplane. The impact of this aircraft on air fighting at the Western Front was such that the German Staff demanded an equivalent without delay, resulting in production of the Fokker Dr I triplane (8), which entered service in August 1917. Perhaps best-known of the many pilots who flew the type was Manfred von Richthofen—the 'Red

Baron'—who was killed eventually while flying the Dr 1 425/17 on 21 April 1918.

Following the Fokker triplane into production was the same company's D VII (9), regarded as one of the best fighter-scout aircraft produced during World War I.

A single-bay biplane, powered by a 160 hp Mercedes D III or 185 hp BMW III six-cylinder in-line liquid-cooled engine, it was armed with two forward-firing Spandau machine-guns. Entering service soon after the death of Manfred von Richthofen, the unit which he had commanded, Geschwader No. 1, was among the first to be equipped with the type.

Proving easy to fly, being highly manoeuvrable and remaining readily controllable even at the operational ceiling of 22,900 ft (6,980 m), the D VII proved to be a formidable opponent. In fact, their potential was regarded so highly by Germany's adversaries that a term of the Armistice Agreement demanded that all Fokker D VII aircraft must be handed over to the Allies.

9

The Wright **Flyer** had been funda-
mentally a dead-end design, offering
no scope for development, but it should
not be thought that the Wrights had held
a monopoly of aircraft design in the
United States. Next in line of succession
was Glenn Curtiss, and because his
original creations had development
potential he should, perhaps, be
regarded as the country's foremost
pioneer. His **June Bug** biplane, powered
by a 40 hp V-8 engine of his own
design, won a trophy on 4 July 1908
after recording a flight of nearly one mile.
Naval aviation may be said to owe its
beginnings to Glenn Curtiss, and the
world's first really practical seaplane was
built and flown by him on 26 June 1911.

Impressed by the products of the
British Avro Company, established by
A. V. Roe, Curtiss paid for an engineer of
that company—B. Douglas Thomas—to
design a tractor biplane for him. This had
evolved by the beginning of World War I
under the designation JN-2.

But it was a development of this
aircraft, the JN-4 **(10)**, which was to be
produced in large numbers. A total of

1,412 JN-4A/Ds were built by the Curtiss Aeroplane & Motor Company, and an additional 1,310 JN-4Ds by other companies. Used as primary trainers the 'Jennies', as they were known affection-ately, not only remained in service use until 1927, but were also the main mount of the first barnstormers, the men who popularized flying throughout the United States.

It has been quoted time and again that development of the aeroplane as a practical vehicle was boosted consider-ably by the two world wars. If by the term aeroplane one implies also its airframe, then this is not strictly true of the first major conflict.

A careful study of the aeroplane's structure which had evolved by 1918 reveals how little had been the effect of four years of combat. It is true that the airframe had advanced beyond the stick-and-string stage—just—but there was little sophistication. Heavy biplane structures, extensively braced and strutted, they demanded a great deal from the power plant, long before

receiving the added weight penalty of a substantial military load. Anthony Fokker commented that these aircraft had built-in headwinds.

The greatest development had come within the field of power plants, but for them to be able to carry aircraft, crew and weapons into the air, they had first to be started: not always a simple procedure.

The traditional method of starting an aircraft's engine was by means of the procedure known as hand swinging. With the ignition system switched off, a mechanic pulls the propeller through by hand to induce a combustible mixture of fuel and air into the cylinders. Then, with ignition on, a sharp pull on the propeller is usually sufficient to encourage the engine into life.

For aircraft like the Avro 504K (11), powered by engines of 100 to 130 hp, hand-swinging was—and very often still is—the only means available for starting the engine.

With more powerful engines it was sometimes possible to start them by

more than one man being involved in the procedure, two or three linking arms to provide a more hefty pull. Another expedient was the rope-and-glove technique, with a canvas glove being slid over one propeller blade. Attached to the canvas was a length of rope, enabling a team of men to give a good strong pull on the propeller for almost 180° of its rotation.

For engines of 200 to 300 hp, like that which powered the F.2A/F.2B Bristol Fighter (12), something rather more positive was necessary. This led to a device known as the Huck's Starter, the original being based on a Model T Ford. A special mechanical arrangement allowed an output shaft to be clutched-in to the engine of the vehicle. This shaft had at one end a metal dog which engaged with a similar dog secured to the propeller boss, allowing the propeller to be spun until the engine fired.

The mobility of the Huck's Starter enabled it to be driven from one aircraft to another, and most airfields soon had one of these indispensable devices available.

12

Between the World Wars

The end of World War 1 brought an appropriate moment for the creation of civil air routes, primarily of a domestic nature, because long range and a worthwhile payload were not then very good travelling companions. The potentially lucrative inter-continental route between London and Paris was perhaps the easiest to bring into being, and was first flown regularly from 8 February 1919. The passengers on these first services were limited to military personnel, as civil aviation had not then been authorized in Britain.

But others were setting their sights on far more ambitious routes than the handful of miles which separated Britain and France. Already there were several teams anxious to be first across the North Atlantic, spurred on by a £10,000 prize offered by the **Daily Mail**. The first private attempt was that made by Harry Hawker and McKenzie Grieve, ending in the ocean some 1,000 miles (1,600 km) from their starting point. Miraculously, they ditched safely near a steamer and both were rescued.

Then, on 14 June 1919, a gravely overloaded Vickers Vimy, crewed by Capt John Alcock and Lt Arthur Whitten-Brown, trundled into the air at St John's, Newfoundland **(13)**, to land 16 hr 27 min later at Clifden, Ireland (Eire). The first non-stop crossing of the North Atlantic had become a reality.

This view of the instrument and control panel of the Vickers Vimy **(14)** will show there was no advanced instrumentation or navigational aids to help Alcock and Brown on their pioneering transatlantic journey.

13

15

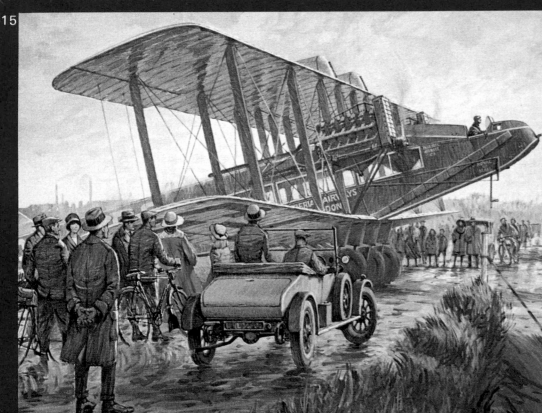

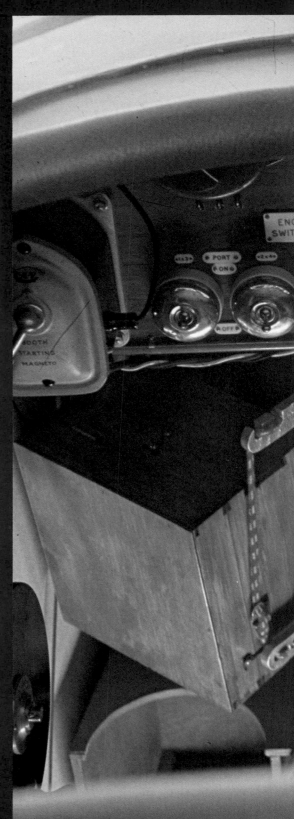

The difficulties were enormous, but these two men had depths of courage sufficient to cope with the hazards they had to face. It was truly an adventurous flight, during which airframe icing nearly forced the Vimy down into the sea. Later, icing of the carburettor air intakes was almost to cut off the supply of life-giving air to the engines, and urgent action was needed to keep the Vimy flying. Five times Brown climbed on to the wing and chipped away the choking ice.

Navigation was by dead reckoning, and having regard to the difficulties experienced during the crossing, was one of supreme accuracy. Only the landing was something of an anti-climax, when an ideal-looking field turned out to be a water-soaked bog, the Vimy nosing-in on touch-down.

But this wartime bomber had suc-ceeded in keeping going, to record the first Atlantic crossing for Alcock and Brown. They not only gained the **Daily Mail** prize, but were elevated to knight-hood by HM King George V.

Soon after the excitement of the Vimy's success had died down, Air Transport & Travel Ltd initiated the first regular London-Paris scheduled passenger service on 25 August 1919, operated from Hounslow aerodrome in a converted de Havilland D.H.4A. Handley Page Transport, flying from Cricklewood, was soon to follow AT & T's lead, utilizing for their service Handley Page 0/400 and V/1500 heavy bombers, which had also been converted for civil use. The other British pioneer airlines were The Instone Air Line and Daimler Airways.

When the latter company began operations on the London-Paris route in April 1922, they were equipped with de Havilland D.H.34s, a specially designed airliner, which could accom-modate nine passengers and carried a steward to serve refreshments.

But it was soon clear that there were nowhere near enough passengers for the British airlines to operate economically, leading to Government intervention and formation of Imperial Airways. This great company was to blaze air lanes around the world, and in so doing created standards of service and safety for others to emulate.

A typical scene of this early period is caught by the skill of artist Kenneth McDonough whose picture **(15)** depicts a Handley Page W.8b Royal Mail airliner of Imperial Airways taxying across Plough Lane, adjacent to Croydon Airport.

16

17

18

Preceding page:

One aeroplane which was to have a great impact on civil aviation was on a very different scale to the 12-seat Handley Page W.8b: namely, the little two-seat Moth designed by Geoffrey de Havilland. Powered by a 60 hp Cirrus engine, this flew for the first time in February 1925.

It was an immediate success, and the Air Ministry ordered it into production for use by flying clubs, this action starting a boom in private and club aviation which spread around the world. Three years later the company developed its own 80 hp Gipsy engine, designed by Frank Halford, which gave the Moth an airspeed of 95 mph (153 km/h).

Then, in the early 1930s, an improved Tiger Moth was evolved, to serve with the RAF from 1932 to 1945 as the standard elementary trainer of Flying Training Command. It remained in service with the RAF Volunteer Reserve until 1951. Many have since become privately owned, and an unusual seaplane conversion is shown in the illustration (16).

The majority of the aircraft types which had been produced until the mid-1930s were of biplane construction. Indeed, at the outbreak of World War II in 1939, many of the world's air forces still retained aircraft of biplane configuration in front line service.

But the first signs of change had become apparent long before 1939. Many of the racing seaplanes designed to participate in the Schneider Trophy Contests were monoplanes, proving that it had become possible to build a clean and comparatively lightweight structure capable of withstanding speed-imposed stresses considerably higher than any experienced by aircraft in civil or military service. To qualify this, the average speed of the world's twelve fastest fighter aircraft was around 166 mph (267 km/h), while the Supermarine S.5 which had won the contest in 1927 had recorded a speed of just over 281 mph (452 km/h).

In Germany, Hugo Junkers had brought to practicality the cantilever monoplane of all-metal construction, using corrugated metal skins to carry some of the structural load. It was but a short step to the Junkers Ju 52/3m (17) of 1931, one of the world's best known transport aircraft.

Utilizing similar constructional techniques to those pioneered by Junkers, the Ford company in America had been a little earlier with a somewhat similar three-engined transport aircraft. The main difference lay in wing configuration, that of the Junkers 52 being low-wing, whilst that of the Ford Tri-motor (18) was high-wing.

It was to prove even more enduring than the Ju 52, and among the pioneering flights achieved by this great aeroplane one must mention the epic flight over the South Pole on 28 November 1929.

Unbelievable though it may seem, it is still possible to find isolated examples of the 'Tin Goose' — as the Tri-motor became known — operating commercial services, which is not too bad for an aircraft evolved in 1926. Many of the transport aircraft of that period took a long time to get from A to B, but their longevity shows clearly that a great deal had been learnt about building durable structures.

This page:

In the United States in 1933 was recorded the maiden flight of a strange looking civil airliner. Strange looking, that is, by comparison with the high-legged corrugated-metal Ford Tri-motor. Known as the Boeing 247 **(19)**, it was to demonstrate also that it was full of strange new ideas. Strange then, perhaps, but they were to revolutionize the design of civil transport aircraft.

A well-streamlined low-wing mono-plane, powered by two engines, it was able to retract its landing gear in flight to reduce drag. Variable pitch propellers gave maximum efficiency for take-off and cruising flight: in emergency the fine pitch setting would allow the Model 247 to climb with full load on the power of only one engine. Trim tabs on the control surfaces brought reduction of aerodynamic loading on control surfaces, enabling an automatic pilot to fly the machine for long periods. And to overcome the old hazard of ice accretion on flying surfaces, a de-icing system was introduced for leading-edges of the wings and tail unit.

When the Boeing 247 entered service with United Air Lines (UAL) in March 1933, it reduced US trans-continental flight time to under 20 hours for the first time. Furthermore, it offered completely new standards of comfort for its ten passengers.

So severe was the impact on the revenue of the competing Trans-continental & Western Air (TWA), that it became essential for them to operate an aircraft that was at least as good if they were to stay in business. The relationship between UAL and the Boeing Company was such that TWA realized it was a waste of time to try and buy from Boeing. Instead, they approached the Douglas Aircraft Company to build a contender for the 247, resulting in the Douglas DC-1 which flew for the first time on 1 July 1933.

The 14-seat DC-2, which followed shortly after, shook the aviation world when one owned by KLM, and flown by Captains Parmentier and Moll, won the handicap section of the London–Melbourne McRobertson Air Race. And in America its successor emerged, the 21-seat Douglas DC-3 **(20)**, destined for immortal fame whether known as DC-3, C-47, Dakota or 'Gooney Bird'. This wonderful aeroplane has served honourably and valiantly, and still continues to serve, with air forces and civil operators around the world.

21

22

21A

While the Douglas DC-3 was busy establishing itself as the champion of US domestic routes, with no less than 80 per cent of all scheduled airlines using the type by December 1941—and recording a 100 per cent safety record during 1939–40—other operators were thinking hard about the Pacific and North Atlantic routes.

Britain's Imperial Airways had pioneered flying-boat services that linked the home country with Australia, India, New Zealand and South Africa, and points between and around. America had concentrated on the Pacific Ocean, a Martin M.130 **China Clipper** recording an inaugural mail flight across the central Pacific from San Francisco to Manila. France and Germany had achieved links between the old and new worlds via the South Atlantic to Rio de Janeiro.

The only stumbling block was the North Atlantic, plagued by weather that posed severe navigational problems and a west-east airstream inimical to all east-west crossings. Although America, Britain and Germany succeeded in flying between Europe and the United States by various experimental means during the 1930s, it remained for America to inaugurate the first regular passenger service across the North Atlantic on

8 July 1939, using 42-ton Boeing Model 314 flying-boats (21).

The use of the expression '42-ton flying-boat' gives little impression of the true size of the Boeing Model 314, known more usually as 'Boeing Clippers'. This resulted from their individual names, such as **Yankee Clipper**, bestowed upon them by Pan American Airways.

A total of twelve were built, six as 314s with 1,500 hp Wright Double Cyclone engines, and a subsequent six 314As with increased passenger accommodation and 1,600 hp engines.

With a crew of 6–10 and a maximum of 77 passengers, the 'Clippers' proved rugged and reliable, both on Atlantic and Pacific routes. Early in World War II three of Pan American's 'boats' were sold to British Overseas Airways Corporation (BOAC), who used them on the Atlantic route throughout the war.

A visual impression of the size of these majestic flying-boats is given by the accompanying photograph (21A) which looks along a part of the 152 ft (46·33 m) wing span.

Simultaneously with the between-wars development of civil aircraft had come similar advances in the military aeroplanes

that equipped the world's air forces.

New standards had been imposed by the seaplanes which had been created to decide final ownership of the Schneider Trophy. In America, the combination of Curtiss D.12 in-line liquid-cooled engine, which reduced frontal area, Curtiss-Reid propeller and streamlined Curtiss racer had so very nearly tipped the scales in their favour.

C. Richard Fairey (later Sir Richard) was so impressed by the D.12 engine that he acquired licence rights to use it, this powering a new aircraft designated Fairey Fox. When demonstrated to the RAF, this day bomber not only proved 50 mph (80 km/h) faster than any other bomber aircraft in service, but could also show a clean pair of heels to any contemporary British fighter. Richard Fairey's far-sightedness shocked designers in the United Kingdom, rather like that from an unexpected bucket of cold water, giving new impetus to the development of more potent fighter and bomber aircraft.

One result was the Hawker Hart (22), which flew for the first time in June 1928. When these aircraft were deployed in the 1930 air exercises they, too, were to prove embarrassing, for the 'defending' Siskin fighters were not fast enough to intercept them.

World War Two

The last biplane fighter to serve with the RAF, the Gloster Gladiator **(23)**, had flown for the first time in September 1934. A fast and highly manoeuvrable single-seat fighter, it virtually represented the ultimate in aerodynamic efficiency for an aircraft of biplane configuration.

In retrospect, it seems strange that Glosters did not utilize a monoplane structure for their private venture project which produced the Gladiator. Their Gloster VI monoplane racing seaplane, built for the 1929 Schneider Trophy Contest, but withdrawn due to engine trouble, had established a little later a world speed record of 336 mph (540 km/h) and demonstrated a maximum speed of 351 mph (565 km/h).

But Glosters were not alone in this respect, for manufacturers the world over seemed reluctant to turn their backs on the biplane configuration which, for so many years, had made it possible to build robust aircraft well able to cope with the stresses and strains of service use.

It was not surprising, of course, that the Fairey Swordfish torpedo-bomber **(24)**, which had flown for the first time in April 1934, was of biplane configuration. With ailerons on both the upper and lower wings, leading-edge slats and generous wing area, the Swordfish was highly manoeuvrable. It had also a wide speed range, between about 50 and 135 mph (80 to 217 km/h), which meant, according to Terence Horsley, author of **Find, Fix and Strike**, that in the Swordfish an "... approach to the carrier deck could be made at stagger-

catering for the higher standards of performance demanded by more far-sighted and realistic military planners, but also that there would no longer be automatic prejudice against a monoplane configuration. The Schneider Trophy Contests, which by 1931 had raised circuit speeds to 340 mph (547 km/h), and the winner of which had set a world speed record of 407 mph (655 km/h), had shown that no longer were drag-inducing configurations necessary to ensure robust structures.

First of these exciting new fighters became named Hurricane **(25)**, originating from the drawing board of Sydney Camm at Hawker Aircraft. It retained the well-known Hawker fuselage structure of fabric-covered tubular steel, and all except early production aircraft had all-metal stressed-skin wings set in a low-wing configuration. Power plant was the Rolls-Royce Merlin, derived from the P.V.12, 'R' and 'sprint' engines which that company had developed to contend the Schneider Trophy.

By the outbreak of World War II, RAF Fighter Command had a total of 18 squadrons of Hurricanes, compared with only 9 squadrons of Spitfires.

Following upon R. J. Mitchell's successful design of the Supermarine S.5, S.6 and S.6B, the trio which had won the Schneider Trophy outright for Britain, it was only to be expected that the company would utilize their hard-earned knowledge to develop a new eight-gun fighter to meet the requirements of the Air Ministry.

26

ingly low speed, yet response to the controls remained firm and insistent. Consider what such qualities meant on a dark night when the carrier's deck was pitching the height of a house."

Known more generally as the 'Stringbag', this was not only a legendary aeroplane in respect of its exploits, but also in terms of longevity, for they were to remain in operational service until after VE-Day, outpacing aircraft which had been built to replace them.

But to even the most unambitious designers it was clear that the days of the biplane were numbered. In continental Europe, Britain and far away America, new sleek lines began to appear as routine on drawing boards. Their originators knew not only that the structures they proposed were capable of

It, too, was designed around the Rolls-Royce Merlin engine, and first flight of the prototype was made on 5 March 1936, some four months after that of the Hurricane. Named Spitfire **(26)**, the first squadron to become equipped with the type in July 1938 was No. 19, based at RAF Duxford.

In the United States there had been no similar development of advanced aircraft. On the contrary, the nation's traditional policy of isolation, plus an acute shortage of funds for the procurement of any new military equipment, had brought stagnation. Furthermore, a long drawn out Army/Navy battle, on the issue of which service was the most able to defend the nation in the event of attack, had produced an atmosphere that was not conducive to the development of anything but ill-feeling.

23

24

25

The United States Army Air Corps (USAAC) retained many devotees of General 'Billy' Mitchell in its ranks. It was this officer who had fallen foul of the establishment by his continued avowal that air power had made sea power obsolescent. Fortunately for America, those who believed in air power were not to be deterred by opposition, and managed eventually to bamboozle a small order for a strategic bomber, having developed a convincing argument to the effect that this particular aircraft was really a defensive weapon.

Built as a private venture by the Boeing Company, their Model 299 prototype flew for the first time on 28 July 1935. Less than a month later, on 20 August 1935, this aircraft made a remarkable 2,100 mile (3,380 km) non-stop flight to Wright Field for its official tests. Then came apparent disaster for Boeing in October, when the 299 crashed on take-off, it being discovered subsequently that the control-locks had not been released before the take-off run.

But the performance of the prototype had been heartening, and eventually 13 aircraft were ordered in January 1936. These were given the designation Y1B-17 when they entered service, between January and August 1937, and one of these early examples is seen in the contemporary colour photograph (27).

Soon after introducing the B-17 Flying Fortress into service, the USAAC planned to demonstrate its capability by 'intercepting' the Italian liner **Rex** 725 miles (1,167 km) out in the Atlantic. The exercise was a great success, three B-17s making a spot-on rendezvous with the liner. Unfortunately, this caused new ill-feeling between Army and Navy, and the USAAC found itself ordered to limit maritime patrols to 100 miles (160 km) offshore. And to cut the air force down to size, it was pointed out quite ruthlessly that the 'enormous' sum spent on a few big and useless bombers was poor planning: a far greater number of small fighter aircraft could have been bought for the same sum.

As a result of the tension created, the procurement of additional urgently needed Flying Fortresses was delayed: to the extent that when the United States realized that strengthening the defence of its Pacific bases was a priority requirement, there were nowhere near sufficient available. In fact, when war in the Pacific seemed inevitable, only 35 B-17s could be deployed there.

It was the Japanese attack on Pearl Harbor, on 7 December 1941, which brought the United States into World War II, and which soon had production lines turning out B-17s (28) like hot cakes. By the war's end, nearly 13,000 had been built.

British bomber procurement had not suffered from the restrictions imposed in the United States. Past experience had left little doubt in the minds of British planners as to the most likely targets, and aircraft like the Vickers Wellington (29), with a range in excess of 2,500 miles (4,023 km) with a 1,000 lb (453 kg) bomb load, had been covered by an Air Ministry specification of 1932. There was also the Armstrong Whitworth Whitley of slightly later vintage, which had a range of 1,650 miles (2,655 km) with 3,000 lb (1,361 kg) of bombs, and the Handley Page Hampden, also of 1932, which could carry 2,000 lb (907 kg) of bombs over a range of 1,885 miles (3,034 km).

It was however the Wellington, known more usually as the 'Wimpey', which proved to be the backbone of Bomber Command in the early years of the war. It retained this position until the first of the long-range four-engined bombers began to enter operational service.

Mk XVI versions could do even better, carrying 4,000 lb (1,814 kg) of bombs.

It was to prove a nightmare for German fighter defences, being too fast to be intercepted, and their loss rate was to prove the lowest of any aircraft utilized by Bomber Command. So successful was the Mosquito bomber, that fighter and reconnaissance versions were very soon put into production.

Meanwhile, in the background, the big four-engined strategic bombers were evolving. In the lead was the Short Stirling, emanating from an Air Ministry specification of 1936. The first successful prototype made its first flight on 3 December 1939.

Next was the Handley Page Halifax, also originating from a 1936 specification, which called for a twin-engined heavy bomber. When the proposed Rolls-Royce Vulture engines were not available, the design was changed to use instead four

29

Seeming very different from any conception of a bomber aircraft was the de Havilland Mosquito (30). Not only did its size suggest that it would carry a bomb-load inferior to that of the slightly larger Bristol Blenheim IV (1,320 lb: 599 kg), but the fact that it was of all-wood construction, had no defensive armament and so relied upon speed to evade airborne adversaries, made it something of a non-starter so far as military planners were concerned.

When the prototype made a demonstration flight, official observers were staggered to discover that it possessed the agility of a fighter, could perform upward rolls on the power of one engine, had a level speed of nearly 400 mph (644 km/h), and could carry a maximum bomb-load of 2,000 lb (907 kg). Later

Rolls-Royce Merlins. Developing successfully, it shared with the Avro Lancaster the major burden of the night offensive against targets in occupied Europe.

Most famous of the three was the Avro Lancaster (31), originating from the unsuccessful twin-engined Avro Manchester, which was also evolved to an Air Ministry specification of 1936. Powered by the new Rolls-Royce Vulture engine, it was withdrawn from service when recurrent trouble with the power plant proved to be a major problem. Like the Halifax, it was redesigned for a four-engine Merlin installation, but was re-named Lancaster. The only British bomber capable of carrying the 22,000 lb 'Grand Slam' bomb, it was of great importance in the latter stages of the war.

32

33

34

Preceding page:

In America, the need for a major strategic bomber had also been recognized by the advanced and dedicated planners of the USAAC. Unfortunately, the procurement of such a weapon was delayed until well beyond the eleventh hour, at a time when even the dumbest of dumb-bunnies was reasonably certain that the US was unlikely to avoid the spread of war taking place in Europe.

It was not until August 1940, after evaluation of competing designs from Boeing, Consolidated, Douglas and Lockheed, that Boeing and Consolidated were instructed to initiate prototype construction.

The Boeing aircraft promised to be the most important, and a mock-up was inspected by the air force in April 1941, at which time the company was urged to make all possible haste with the two XB-29 prototypes. Almost simultaneously a test batch of 14 YB-29s were ordered, and production contracts for 250 B-29s **(32)** were placed in September 1941, an additional 250 in January 1942, and in excess of 1,000 more by September 1942. Never had such large orders been placed for an unproven aircraft, the first prototype of which did not fly until 21 September 1942.

In fact, the B-29 was very different from any aircraft which had been planned before. Not only was it required to carry a 2,000 lb (907 kg) bomb-load over a range of 5,333 miles (8,583 km), it was expected also to do this at a speed of 400 mph (644 km/h). In addition, armour protection, self-sealing fuel tanks, heavy defensive armament and the ability to uplift a 16,000 lb (7,257 kg) bomb-load over a shorter range were requirements of the specification.

When the B-29A entered service, it could demonstrate a range of 5,380 miles (8,658 kg), a maximum bomb-load of 20,000 lb (9,072 kg), and met the requirements in respect of armour protection and self-sealing tanks. Defensive armament comprised up to twelve 0·50-in machine-guns and one 37 mm cannon.

The accompanying illustrations **(33, 34)** give some appreciation of the size of this aeroplane, production of which became the largest single aircraft programme of World War II.

This page:

Like air forces around the world, that of the United States retained aircraft of biplane configuration for primary flying training. One of the most popular in America was the Stearman Kaydet **(35)**, first produced as a private venture by the Stearman Aircraft Corporation in 1934. Although Army reaction was slow initially, a total of almost 5,000 were built for the air force, in addition to others for the US Navy and for export. Power plant of the Kaydet's many versions differed somewhat, ranging from a 215 hp Lycoming R-680-5 to a 280 hp R-680-11.

For a primary flying training role the biplane proved ideal, being extremely manoeuvrable and with a high degree of controllability, even at low flying speeds. This meant that pupil pilots could make their first approaches and landings at speeds which gave them time to think.

While the European nations were busy preparing for World War II, a conflict which seemed inevitable having regard to events in continental Europe, the isolationist policy of the United States was still very much to the fore.

In the long-drawn-out battle between Army and Navy, it was the latter service which was able to exert the most influence on military policy decisions. In consequence, there had been a tendency for the Army to have to make do with the equipment it possessed. Naval planners considered that they could ensure the security of America's coastline, and with no national intention of joining in other people's quarrels, there was no real need for the Army to have any very startling attack aircraft. The only real danger to America lay in the Far East, which meant that procurement policy was concerned primarily with long-range transport, bombardment and logistic support.

In Europe, short- and medium-range aircraft were the most vital concern, particularly fighters and medium-range fast bombers. And when it seemed that national production capacity was likely to prove inadequate, both France and Britain turned to American manufacturers.

As a result of this approach, US designers and engineers began to produce new generations of aircraft, often sub-contracting production to other companies when their own capacity was at full-stretch. Thus, Boeing at Seattle was able to boast a line up of Douglas A-20s **(36)**.

36

The Douglas A-20 was an original design, but by the time the US Army placed its first contract in July 1939, production of several hundred of these aircraft for the French and British air forces was well under way.

In RAF service this aircraft is well remembered as the Boston (37), the original Boston Is serving as trainers, while Boston IIs were all converted as Havocs for the night fighter or intruder role. Boston IIIs, IVs and Vs served as light day-bombers, many replacing Blenheims in squadron service.

By direct purchase, and later by Lend-Lease, many US aircraft came into RAF use, including the Brewster Buffalo, Boeing Flying Fortress, Consolidated Catalina and Liberator, Curtiss Tomahawk and Kittyhawk, Douglas Dakota, Lockheed Hudson and Ventura, Martin Baltimore and Marauder, and North American Harvard, Mitchell and Mustang, amongst others.

The Mustang was of particular interest, for this was not merely an anglicized version of an existing type, but was designed to meet a British specification for an eight-gun fighter. It was to prove a vital aircraft to the United States Army Air Force (USAAF) in the European theatre, particularly when long-range fighters were needed to escort 8th Air Force bombers on daylight sorties that penetrated deep into enemy-held territory.

Germany had long been preparing for war in Europe, building up an air force, training its personnel in Russia.

The primary task envisaged for this air force—the Luftwaffe—was to be what we then called an Army co-operation role; today, such operations would be classed as close-support. Working closely in conjunction with, and acting as the spearhead of, fast-moving, well-armed and armoured ground forces, it was considered that this combination would prove to be the most effective for the kind of war which would be fought in Europe.

German participation in the Spanish Civil War showed that this concept was right, and provided a wonderful opportunity for the testing of weapons and military techniques under real operational conditions.

Among the first German machines to see service in Spain was the Messerschmitt Me 109 (38), designed by Willy Messerschmitt, and now regarded as probably the most outstanding German fighter aircraft of all time.

Like the Supermarine Spitfire, it was to remain in front-line service throughout the European phase of the war, and was developed progressively from the 254 mph (570 km/h), and 36,100 ft (11,000 m) service ceiling of the Me 109E, first major production version, to the 452 mph (727 km/h) and 41,000 ft (12,500 m) service ceiling of the Me 109K.

Both the Hurricane and Spitfire were powered by the Rolls-Royce Merlin in-line liquid-cooled engine. The small frontal area of this type of engine offered advantages for high-speed fighter aircraft, and it is significant that four great fighters —Hurricane, Spitfire, Me 109 and Mustang—all had in-line engines.

There were two notable exceptions, both conspicuously successful aircraft, which had radial air-cooled engines: the

38

39

German Focke-Wulf Fw 190 and Japanese Mitsubishi A6M Zero.

Before the war America had concentrated on the development of powerful and reliable radial air-cooled engines, accounting for the rather barrel-shaped appearance of many of her early wartime aircraft, including products of Boeing, Brewster, Curtiss, Grumman and Seversky. Some of these aircraft, and particularly those intended for US Navy service, were designed to have a dive-bombing capability.

Germany's Junkers Ju 87 **Stuka** dive-bomber (39) is reputed to have originated because Germany's Ernst Udet had been so impressed by American dive-bombing techniques. When first introduced into action in the Spanish Civil War the performance of the Ju 87 had not been impressive. When used in conjunction with armoured columns the **Blitzkrieg** was born, and Stukas spearheaded the attacks in Poland and France, the scream of their wind-driven sirens adding to the terror and confusion they caused, particularly to columns of civilian refugees.

German aircraft such as the Junkers Ju 87 and Messerschmitt Me 109 had been developed clandestinely, their pilots training at the Luftwaffe's pre-war base in Russia.

Bomber aircraft, such as the Dornier Do 17 and Heinkel He 111 cut their teeth in Lufthansa service, both ostensibly high-speed transport aircraft. Their use on Lufthansa international routes provided excellent crew training, with services to London and Paris allowing familiarization over routes which would one day have to be flown under far more difficult conditions.

The Heinkel He 111 (40), powered by Daimler-Benz engines, was well known to the citizens of Britain during 1940–41, the note of its unsynchronized engines remembered still, and especially by those who lived in Birmingham, Coventry and London. It remained in service throughout the war, although gradually becoming obsolete, but was able to record a wide range of activities. These included torpedo-bomber, pathfinder, glider tug, V-1 missile launcher, paratroop and cargo transport.

37

40

Ernst Heinkel was not concerned only with conventional aircraft, such as the He III, but was both far-sighted and unafraid to experiment. Learning of the research on jet propulsion being carried out by Dr Pabst von Ohain at Göttingen University, he engaged the doctor and his assistant, Max Hahn, to continue their experiments at Marienehe. By September 1937 von Ohain was bench-running a hydrogen-fuelled turbojet engine, but although he was unaware of it, Frank Whittle in England had attained this goal five months earlier.

It was, however, the combined efforts of von Ohain and Heinkel that recorded the world's first flight of a turbojet-powered aircraft, when the Heinkel He 178 powered by an HeS 3b engine made its first successful flight on 27 August 1939.

Despite this early lead, it was not until almost three years later, on 18 July

1942, that the prototype of Germany's first operational turbojet aircraft, the Messerschmitt Me 262, made its maiden flight. There were to be further delays before it entered service, for Adolf Hitler insisted it should be developed as a fighter-bomber, and it was not until 3 October 1944 that the first unit began operations. The Me 262 **(41)** illustrated is in the Museum at Munich, surrounded by aircraft of other ages.

Development of a British turbojet-powered aircraft was to occupy a very similar time scale. Although Frank Whittle (later Sir Frank) had run the world's first aircraft turbojet engine on 12 April 1937, it was not until March 1938 that he received an Air Ministry contract to produce a flight engine.

The airframe to be wedded with this power plant was contracted with the

Gloster Aircraft Company on 3 February 1940, designated by its AM specification number E.28/39. This flew for the first time at RAF Cranwell, on the evening of 15 May 1941, and proved to be a remarkably trouble-free machine considering the experimental nature of both engine and airframe.

At this time the German industry had a lead of 21 months, but before the E.28/39 had flown Glosters had already received an order for 12 twin-engined fighters to Air Ministry Specification F.9/40. Named Meteor **(42)**, the fifth prototype (DG206/G) was to record the first flight of the type on 5 March 1943, and they began to equip the RAF's No. 616 Squadron on 12 July 1944. Meteors became operational in August with 616 Squadron, and recorded their first 'kill' of a V-1 flying bomb on 4 August 1944.

Post-War Civil, Military & Light Aircraft

By the time that the jet-fighters had become established in service, the war in Europe was in its closing stages. In the Far East the Americans had been fighting their way towards Japan. When the giant B-29s became available in quantity they began to destroy Japanese industry by devastating incendiary attacks. And it was the B-29s that were to drop the only two atomic bombs used operationally. The first, carried by the B-29 **Enola Gay**, was dropped over Hiroshima on 6 August 1945. Three days later the B-29 **Bock's Car** dropped the second weapon over Nagasaki. On 14 August 1945 the Japanese surrendered, and World War II had ended.

It was realized that there would be a tremendous upsurge in civil aviation, for during the war thousands of men had learned to fly, and millions of men and women had come to accept air travel as routine.

The circumstances of war had put America in a position to make the most of the situation, for her aircraft industry had been forced to specialize in the construction of long-range bomber and transport aircraft.

Boeing, for example, had designed in 1942 a military transport which became designated C-97 Stratofreighter. Its introduction was delayed by the need to concentrate on Boeing B-29 production, but between 1947 and 1949 56 civil airliner versions of the C-97 were built. Designated as the Model 377 Stratocruiser **(43)**, these introduced post-war inter-continental travellers to undreamed of standards of comfort and service.

Another American manufacturer to find it was in an excellent post-war situation was Lockheed. Just before the beginning of the war the company had designed a four-engined inter-continental transport aircraft to a specification issued by Transcontinental & Western Air (TWA), subsequently Trans World Airlines.

Designated originally as the L-49 project, the aircraft eventually became named Constellation and was ordered by both TWA and Pan American, though the latter company decided at a later stage to limit its Constellations and to concentrate on the Boeing Stratocruiser.

Before the prototype L-49 was completed America was at war, and as the C-69 the Constellation was called up

44

40

for military service. Its use was primarily as a 63-seat troop transport, and it was not until the end of 1945 that TWA began to receive its civil 'Connies'.

Transatlantic services to the UK were started by Pan American on 4 February 1946 and by TWA on the following day, both using the Model L-049. Illustrated **(44)** are the L-1049C Super Connie (Qantas), the first civil version with turbo-compound engines, and the much larger L-1649 Starliner which entered service in 1957.

Aircraft such as the L-1649, and the Douglas Company's DC-7C, represented the peak of development of the piston-engined commercial airliner.

The UK had not been in the same league as the Americans when it came to post-war civil airliners. Instead of the comparatively smooth transition of purpose-built transport from military austerity to civil luxury, Britain had to make do with hasty conversions of wartime bombers. Not surprisingly, they could not compare with such aircraft as the Boeing Stratocruiser, Douglas DC-4 and Lockheed Constellation. Furthermore, prior to the war BOAC had operated her long-range Commonwealth routes with flying-boats that offered superb standards of comfort. Six years later these aircraft could not compete economically with the long-range landplanes developed to satisfy military requirements. Very soon BOAC was losing traffic to the US airlines, and had to buy Constellations and Stratocruisers to stay in business.

But Britain had one ace up her sleeve: a distinct lead in turbine engine technology, and the de Havilland Company set about building a civil airliner around four of these power plants. The resulting Comet 1 began the world's first jet-airliner service on 2 May 1952, to Johannesburg, and it seemed the British aircraft industry had a world-beater on its hands. Then came the tragic loss of three Comet 1s. Painstaking detective work by scientists and engineers was to prove that metal fatigue had brought about disintegration of the pressurized cabin.

It was not until 4 October 1958 that BOAC was able to renew transatlantic services with the Comet 4 **(45)**, developed by de Havilland to overcome the structural failure of the Comet 1: but by then, Britain had already lost her design lead.

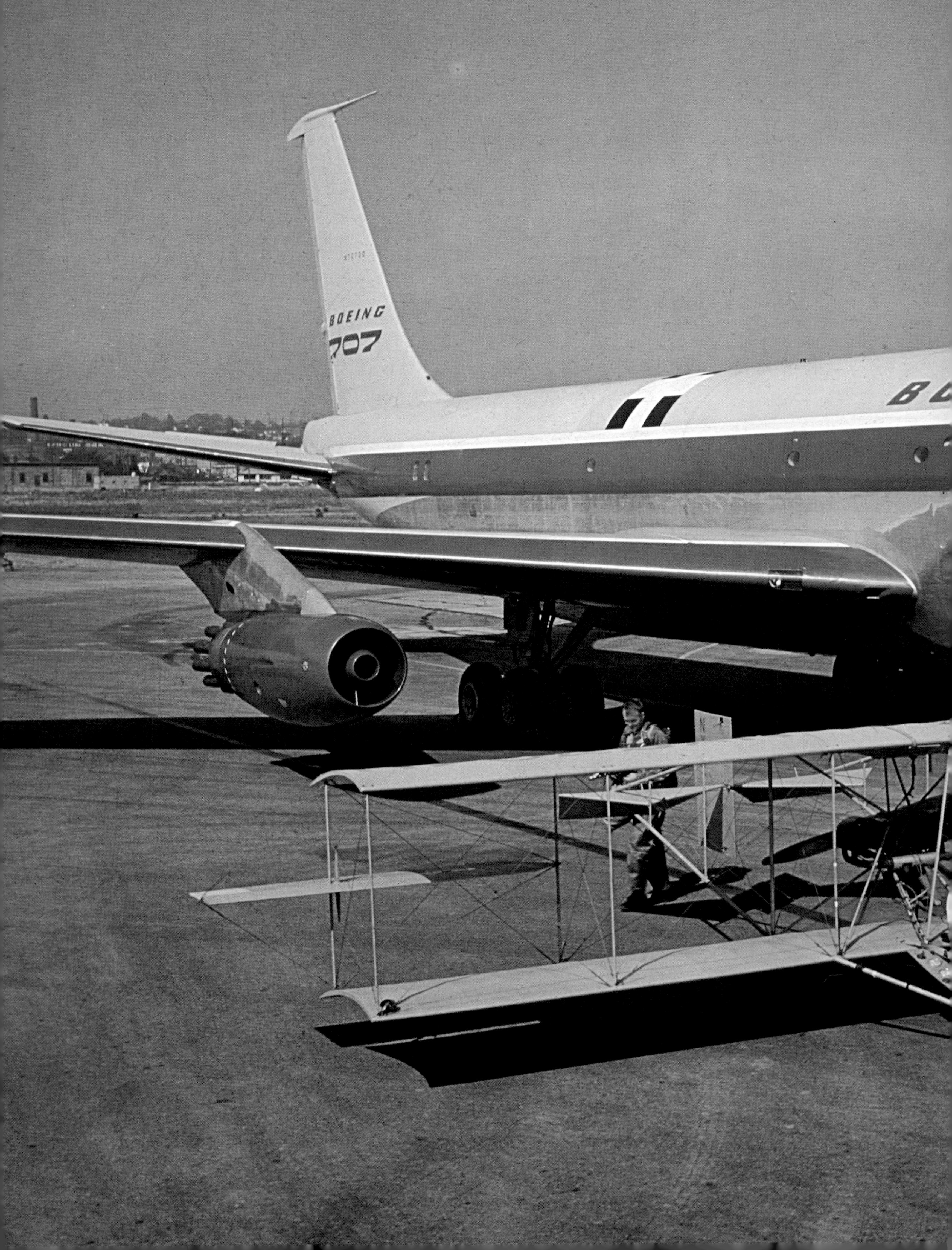
BOEING
707

Preceding page:

The American industry, very busy supplying piston-engined airliners to satisfy a huge world market, had not so much incentive to speed the development of turbine-engined transports. So it was not until 15 July 1954 that the Boeing Company flew the prototype of their Model 367-80, a remarkable four-engined transport, which has since become known the world over under the designation of Boeing 707.

But this aircraft had been developed initially as a flight refuelling tanker for the United States Air Force (USAF), and it was not until two years after the first flight of the 'Dash Eighty'—as the prototype is known affectionately to all Boeing employees—that the USAF gave permission for commercial development.

Pan American were to record the first transatlantic flight with the 707 on 26 October 1958, and when the longer-range 707-320 Inter-continental became available in 1959, it very soon found employment in the service of the major airlines of the world. A lighter-weight shorter-range version designated Boeing 720 entered service with United Air Lines (UAL) on 5 July 1960, and as a measure of success it can be recorded that no fewer than 895 Boeing 707/720s had been delivered by 1 June 1975.

Our picture **(46)** shows the 'Dash-Eighty' prototype with Peter Bowers' Curtiss replica in the foreground.

This page:

It should not be thought, of course, that introduction of turbine power plants had eliminated the piston-engine from the aviation scene. Years of development have ensured that modern engines of this type are both reliable and efficient: the turbojet scores for power and speed, but is by comparison a fuel-thirsty engine.

It must be remembered also that there are far less glamorous roles for civil aircraft than prestige inter-continental services: there is also the bread-and-butter job of carrying air cargo, an ever-expanding market in the post-war years.

The Bristol Aeroplane Company were to build a far from beautiful but successful aircraft for this role, the prototype of their Type 170 Freighter and Wayfarer (G-AGPV) making its first flight on 2 December 1945, powered by two Bristol Hercules engines. These aircraft were to provide valuable and reliable

47

48

service to their users, employed on a wide variety of tasks, and will be remembered especially for their cross-Channel car ferry role with Silver City Airways. Illustrated is the final version, the Super Freighter (47), developed at the instigation of Silver City.

There were also many military requirements that could be satisfied effectively by piston-engined aircraft, particularly for primary trainers and lightweight communications aircraft.

Typical of this latter category is the Hunting Percival Pembroke (48), which replaced the veteran Avro Anson in some RAF Communication Flights in 1953. Its two 540/560 hp Alvis Leonides piston-engines made it economical to operate, and mounting of the engines on the high wing, coupled with tricycle landing gear, made the type very suitable for operation from unimproved airstrips.

With rearward-facing seating for eight passengers, it has proved valuable not only for the communications role but, like the Anson before it, was readily convertible to a 'flying classroom' for the training of air signallers and navigators.

For the British aircraft industry the failure of the Comet 1 had come as a serious and crippling blow in the attempt to gain world markets for civil aircraft.

It was fortunate that they had a second string to their bow, evolving from another pioneering project aimed at achieving greater economy from turbine power plants. Known as a turboprop engine, this retains a turbine as its heart, but drives a conventional propeller through the medium of reduction gearing. The result is economical operation—by comparison with a pure turbojet—while retaining the unique smoothness of an engine devoid of reciprocating parts.

The first combination of this type of engine and a civil airliner came with the Vickers Viscount, and the supply of 60 of these aircraft to Capitol Airlines of America represented the first major sale of a British civil transport into the American market. Typical of many excellent turbo-prop airliners is the Dutch medium-sized short/medium-range Fokker-VFW F.27 Friendship (49). Still in production, over 21 years after the first flight of the prototype, the F.27 has been 'stretched' progressively from a 28-seater to a 48-seater.

Britain's Viscount was a distinct success, and was followed by the larger Bristol Britannia which entered service on BOAC's London–Johannesburg route on 1 February 1957. The Britannia, which must surely rank as one of the most graceful post-war aircraft, was to prove another success for British industry.

Vickers, meanwhile, were busy on the development of an aircraft of Britannia size, a demand spurred by both BEA and Trans-Canada Air Lines, resulting in the Vanguard (50) with Rolls-Royce Tyne turboprop engines. The prototype flew for the first time on 20 January 1959, but it was not until just over two years later that the first Type 951 Vanguards went into service with BEA.

The majority of the Vanguards remaining in service have since been converted to serve as cargo aircraft, those which were in Air Canada (successor to TCA) service being known as Cargoliners, while those of BEA are known as Merchantmen.

50

Very much in the same size category as the highly successful Viscount was the product of another well-known British company. This was the Handley Page Herald (51), which was, however, powered by only two Rolls-Royce Dart turboprop engines.

But the prototype of the Dart-engined Herald flew for the first time on 11 March 1958, almost ten years after the first flight of the Viscount. What, then, were the market hopes for such an aircraft? Was it not ten years too late?

Indeed no. The Herald is used to illustrate that two aircraft of a similar size can be built to satisfy quite different requirements. The Viscount was for conventional airline service, its low-wing configuration providing easier refuelling and servicing, a better chance of survival if the aircraft had to be ditched, and allowed also the use of a lighter weight landing gear structure.

The Herald was intended for civil or military service, operating from all types of airfields. Thus the high-wing setting gave greater clearance between ground and propeller, reducing the likelihood of damage; the high landing gear allowed the use of long shock-struts, giving a smoother ride on undeveloped strips; and the underslung fuselage made loading and unloading easy without a need for sophisticated ground equipment.

In Russia a requirement to transport large volumes of both civil and military cargo over long distances has speeded the development of large transport aircraft.

The An-22 Antheus **(52)** represents the solution offered by Oleg Antonov's bureau, design studies originating in 1962 and the prototype making its first flight on 27 February 1965.

When displayed at the Paris Air Show, on 15 June 1965, it came as something of a surprise to the Western World. Certainly everything is on a large scale, for the wings span 211 ft 4 in (64·40 m), its contra-rotating propellers are 20 ft 4 in (6·20 m) in diameter, and each main landing gear unit comprises three pairs of levered suspension units.

Four 15,000 shp Kuznetsov turboprop engines allow the giant to lift-off at a gross weight of 551,160 lb (250,000 kg) — about 245 tons — and carry a payload of 176,350 lb (80,000 kg) — almost 80 tons — over a range of 3,100 miles (5,000 km).

52

54

ROYAL NEPAL AIRLINES

Following the initial success of the Comet 1, the resurgent French industry joined battle by designing a short/medium-range airliner which was to acquire the name Caravelle.

It differed from the ideas or hardware of other countries in one important respect, it introduced rear-mounted turbojet engines, with a Rolls-Royce Avon on each side of the aft fuselage.

What advantage did this arrangement offer? At the stage of the art it permitted a cleaner and more efficient wing, improved take-off performance and last, but by far from least, a quieter cabin environment.

Designed by the French company Sud-Ouest (subsequently Sud-Aviation, and now Aérospatiale as a result of industry mergers), a prototype flew for the first time on 27 May 1955, and Caravelle Is entered service with Air France and SAS in mid-1959. Illustrated are Caravelle IIIs **(53)** of Air Charter International.

At about the same time that the Caravelle first entered airline service, Boeing in America began design studies of a short/medium-range airliner. Similar in appearance to the highly successful 707—and with a commonality of many parts—it had been decided that to achieve the most economic operation factors it was necessary to reduce from four to three engines. As an asymmetric layout was quite impractical, it was decided to rear-mount the three engines: one on each side of the rear fuselage, the third at the base of the T-tail assembly. Thus, a second rear-engined aircraft came into service, but for different reasons.

Flown for the first time on 9 February 1963, 727-100s entered scheduled service with Eastern Air Lines on 1 February 1964. Just over 11 years later, on 1 June 1975, the amazing total of 1,132 Boeing 727s **(54)** had been delivered to the world's airlines.

55

In Britain, Vickers had watched the Caravelle with interest, for they were considering such a layout for a military project. Then came a BEA requirement for a short/medium-range transport, leading to design studies of a Vanguard type fuselage with three rear-mounted engines. Finally, BOAC came into the picture, requiring a long-range transport with greater payload, so the choice was made to use four Rolls-Royce Conway turbofan engines, but still in a rear-mounted configuration.

Why rear-mounted for Vickers? The requisite range and payload meant that a thinner-section more efficient wing was desirable. If it was required to serve as the mounting for four engines, then it could not be such an efficient aerofoil. Vickers also favoured the rear-mounted layout to give better airfield performance, lower approach speeds, improved control characteristics, reduced fire hazards in a crash landing, reduced risk of damage from runway debris and, of course, a lower cabin noise level.

The VC10, as the type became named, entered airline service with BOAC on 29 April 1964, proving an immediate success. The 'stretched'-fuselage increased-payload Super VC10 **(55)** began scheduled operations on 1 April 1965.

Before turning away, for the moment, from civil transport aircraft, it is interesting to note how The Boeing Company has followed a logical train of evolution, ranging from the long-range four-engined 707/720, to the short/medium-range 727, and leading to the decision to produce also a twin-engined short-haul version of the same basic configuration, this becoming designated 737 **(56)**.

Since only two engines were required, allowing symmetric disposition, a return to the wing-mounted configuration of the 707 was chosen. And although there has been a reduction in structural weight and overall length, there is still a commonality of components with both the 707 and 727, offering valuable production—and spares stockholding—economies.

The first 737-100 entered service with Lufthansa on 10 February 1968, and a total of 414 had been delivered by 1 June 1975. Some slight measure of Boeing's vast experience in the manufacture of large aircraft is given by the fact that the company's 2,500th commercial jet transport was delivered—to Transavia of the Netherlands—on 17 May 1974.

58

Not very long after the end of World War II, in mid-1948 to be more precise, the temperature of the Cold War between East and West dropped an alarming number of degrees. It was occasioned by the Soviet Union closing surface routes to Berlin, signalling the beginning of the historic Berlin Airlift.

During the eleven months duration of this attempt to force the occupying American, British and French troops out of the German capital, the entire population of West Berlin—some two million people—plus the occupying forces, were sustained from the air. Even bulk supplies of such materials as flour and coal were carried in vast quantities, but barrels of petrol were considered far from ideal loads by the crews involved.

USAF transport aircraft were heavily engaged: the C47, our old friend the DC-3 in military guise; the C-54 Sky-master, a military version of the Douglas DC-4; the C-74 Globemaster, a develop-ment of the C-54; and the Fairchild C-82 Flying Boxcar, the only one of the four designed especially as a military transport. This experience showed the need for purpose-built heavy transport aircraft, and among the first to be evolved was the Douglas C-124 Globemaster II **(57)**, based on the C-74, and similarly powered with radial air-cooled engines. Large cargo volume was provided by the aircraft's deep fuselage, and clam-shell nose loading doors and a built-in ramp facilitated the rapid loading of cargo.

Fairchild's C-123 Provider **(58)** bore no relationship to the same company's Flying Boxcar. Instead, it evolved from a cargo glider designed by Chase Aircraft in 1949. When flown by that company as a powered aircraft, in April 1951, it became designated XC-123A.

Two years later, when Chase had been acquired by the Kaiser-Frazer Corporation, the USAF cancelled the contract for its production and gave it, instead, to Fairchild. This forward-looking company immediately began development of the basic design, introducing a large dorsal fin, and some examples had wider-track landing gear for improved stability on the ground and underwing pod-mounted auxiliary turbojet engines to augment the output of the conventional piston-engines.

Many C-123s served in Vietnam for the airlift of troops and cargo. Some, like the one illustrated, were transferred into the service of the Vietnam Air Force.

With the introduction of turboprop engines to civil transport aircraft, demonstrating daily the many advantages of turbine power plants, it was inevitable that the USAF would soon specify this power source for future military transports.

This moment came with the issue of a specification for a Logistic Carrier Supporting System, and the Douglas Aircraft Company's design was ordered into production for the Military Air Transport Service (MATS). Designated C-133 Cargomaster **(59)**, the first of these was delivered to MATS on 29 August 1957.

Later production versions had four 6,500 shp Pratt & Whitney T34-P-7WA turboprop engines, the gross take-off and landing weight of these aircraft being 282,000 lb (127,913 kg). They accom-modate a crew of ten, plus 200 troops and their equipment, or 13,000 cu ft (368·12 m^3) of cargo. Special clam-shell rear doors permit the carriage of operational Inter-continental Ballistic Missiles (ICBMs) without the need to disassemble them.

57

59

Lockheed's C-130 Hercules had been designed to meet the same turboprop transport requirement as the Douglas C-133. They serve the USAF in a wide variety of roles, including the conventional transport of troops and cargo, with DC-130Es for Remotely Piloted Vehicle (RPV) launch and control; WC-130Es for weather reconnaissance; KC-130Fs with flight refuelling capability; HC-130Hs for air search, rescue and recovery; HC-130Ns for the recovery of space capsules; KC-130R tankers; and LC-130Rs with wheel/ski landing gear for Arctic operations. C-130 Hercules served many other air forces throughout the world.

Lockheed followed with the C-141 StarLifter, a four-turbofan transport which went into operational service with MATS (now Military Airlift Command: MAC) on 23 April 1965. MAC's 14 C-141 squadrons comprised the primary airlift capability in 1971, providing supplies to US forces in Vietnam on a daily basis.

Grand-daddy of them all, of course, is Lockheed's C-5A Galaxy **(60)** with four 41,100 lb thrust General Electric turbofan engines, 220,967 lb (100,228 kg) payload, and maximum range with this payload of 3,749 miles (6,033 km).

All this talk about long-range civil and military transports of landplane configuration should not suggest that water-borne aircraft no longer exist, nor that attempts to develop new aircraft within this category died a natural death immediately after World War II.

Prior to the war the German company of Dornier had developed a particularly graceful three-engined flying-boat, the Do 24, the first prototype of which (D-ADLR) flew for the first time on 3 July 1937. Built by various manufacturers, they performed valuable wartime service on sea-air rescues.

Spain acquired twelve of these aircraft in 1944 for sea-air rescue in the Mediterranean. Designated HR.5, some continue in service, as shown by the aircraft on the right of the illustration **(61)**. That filling the background of the picture is a Grumman Albatross, which is of rather later vintage.

The Glenn L. Martin Company of Baltimore, Maryland, had been building aircraft for the US Navy since the early 1920s. In 1937 they began design of a new flying-boat which was to be contemporary with the Consolidated PBY Catalina, many of which served with the British Royal Air Force during World War II. One of their best remembered actions was that performed by Catalinas of Coastal Command's Nos. 209 and 240 Squadrons, which respectively spotted and shadowed the German battleship **Bismarck** after naval forces had lost contact.

Martin's new 'boat, the PBM Mariner **(62)**, first went into service during 1941. Most were employed on long-range maritime patrol or anti-submarine warfare (ASW), but twenty were equipped as 20-seat transports with standardized British/US equipment. A large number, of course, were used for sea-air rescue duties, and of the 631 built many continued in this role for twenty years. The Mariner will always be remembered for its graceful appearance, and was easily recognized by its gull-wing and inward-canted endplate fins.

But the days of water-borne aircraft were virtually numbered so far as long-range transport was concerned. Aircraft like Britain's post-war Saunders-Roe Princesses were cocooned and forgotten while awaiting more powerful engines that would convert them into Queens of the air. By the time that suitable engines were available, economists had proved that landplanes could accomplish the same duties faster and more cheaply.

Flying-boats for maritime patrol were to remain in service for some years, but specialized adaptations of landplanes had proved more versatile. Navies investigated a number of water-borne craft, such as the Convair Sea Dart for a strike role and various flying-boats as transports.

One ambitious project was the Martin

As the war neared its end, high-speed aircraft began to be challenged by a new enemy, one called compressibility. Pilots of high-performance fighters, such as the American P-38 Lightning and British Typhoon, had discovered that when approaching maximum speed in a dive their aircraft would often shudder violently. This was sometimes so severe that wings and tail units broke away from the main structure and many pilots lost their lives.

By testing models in supersonic (faster than sound) wind tunnels, aerodynamicists discovered that as the speed of sound was approached the previously smooth airflow over the wings began to break up into shock waves, causing the violent buffeting. Solution of the problem was speeded post-war when Allied

64

P6M SeaMaster **(63)**, surely the most advanced flying-boat ever built. Intended to fulfil a mine-laying and reconnaissance role, this 100 ft (30·48 m) span all-metal craft had a swept monoplane wing, with four turbojet engines mounted in pairs in nacelles on the upper surface of the wing. Its combat radius of 1,500 miles (2,415 km) could be extended by flight refuelling, and other advanced features included a pressurized flight deck and ejection seats for all four crew members.

Although the SeaMaster was capable of a speed in excess of 600 mph (960 km/h), service trials established that newly developing carrier-based aircraft had virtually outdated those which operated independently from the surface of the sea.

scientific teams found documents which showed German researchers had discovered that thin-section swept wings (i.e. with the leading-edge of the wing forming an angle of less than 90° to the rear of the fuselage) could delay the onset of buffeting.

The Bell Aircraft Company was requested to build for the USAF a series of robust rocket-engined research aircraft. Flown by Major Charles 'Chuck' Yeager, the X-1 was the first to exceed the speed of sound in October 1947. Later, in 1953, he flew the X-1A **(64)** at 1,650 mph (2,655 km/h), proving that a properly designed aircraft would have no difficulty in entering the regime of supersonic flight.

66

Preceding page:

As research continued, the problems of flight at speeds in excess of Mach 1 (the speed of sound, approx 760 mph: 1,223 km/h at sea level) faded into the background. It was no longer a question of building an aircraft to slip cleanly from subsonic to supersonic flight, but how to cope with the airframe temperatures generated by kinetic heating as speeds climbed higher and higher. It was to be overcome by using titanium and stainless steel construction, the airframe 'skinned' with Iconel X nickel alloy steel to withstand temperatures ranging from +1,200°F to −300°F. When temperatures in excess of this upper limit were encountered it became necessary to cover the entire airframe with an ablative coating, like a missile's nose-cone, which burns away at about 530°F to maintain the temperature of the structure well below the design figure of 1,200°F.

Last of the rocket-engined aircraft, which terminated the high-speed research programme, was the North American X-15-A2 **(65)** which, in October 1967, carried Major 'Pete' Knight of the USAF more than fifty miles above the Earth's surface, earning him an astronaut's wings. More than that, it flashed him through the air at an almost unbelievable 4,534 mph (7,297 km/h), before he made a conventional—if fast—landing.

Design of a high-performance turbojet-powered fighter for the USAF had begun in 1944. But as we have already seen, German research had shown that swept wings were vital for high speeds and structural integrity.

It was decided, despite the inevitable delay, to redesign this fighter to incorporate such wings, and it was not until 1 October 1947 that the prototype of this new North American fighter took to the air, to be designated eventually as the North American F-86 Sabre **(66)**.

Within days of that flight, 'Chuck' Yeager had confirmed that a robust swept-wing design could exceed the speed of sound, and in the Spring of 1948 the Sabre exceeded Mach 1 in a shallow dive, the first USAF fighter to do so.

Communist plans having failed to make any headway with the confrontation on West Berlin, the next move was war in Korea. Here the Sabre was to win high esteem when in combat with Russian MiG-15 jet-fighters. The first recorded combats came on 17 December 1950, when four MiGs were destroyed.

Major variants of the F-86 included the F-86F with modified wing leading-edge to improve high-altitude manoeuvrability (2,540 built) and F-86D all-weather fighter (2,504 built). Many F-86Ks, also an all-weather fighter, served with NATO units in Europe. Though no longer serving with the USAF, they still equip some 20 of the world's air forces.

68

69

The USAF's first multi-seat all-weather interceptor-fighter, the Northrop F-89 Scorpion, entered service in July 1950.

Intended as a home defence weapon for utilization by Air Defence Command (ADC), the Scorpion was powered by two turbojets which in the F-89D version gave an initial rate of climb of 8,360 ft (2,548 m)/minute—more than 1½ miles (2·4 km) a minute! Service ceiling was 49,200 ft (14,995 m).

The F-89D was certainly a potent weapon, for it carried an armament of twenty-six 2·75 in folding-fin rockets in a pod on each wingtip. The illustration (67) shows test firing of these rockets over the Californian desert during the summer of 1952.

This page:

Forty-five degrees of wing sweepback was responsible for North American's private-venture fighter being known as the Sabre 45. It had been developed from the highly successful F-86 Sabre, but was two years in project design before the company were awarded a USAF contract for two YF-100 prototypes.

It emerged as a sleek-looking aeroplane, the first of the USAF's 'Century-Series' fighters (F-100 and upwards), and the first operational fighter in the world capable of supersonic speed in level flight. It was used to set a new world speed record of 755·149 mph (1,215·29 km/h) on 29 October 1953.

Designated as the F-100 Super Sabre (68) they began to equip Tactical Air Command (TAC) in late November 1953. F-100Cs could carry a total of 6,000 lb (2,721 kg) of weapons on underwing hard points and demonstrated a speed of Mach 1·25. On 20 August 1955 one of these aircraft raised the world speed record yet again, this time to 822·135 mph (1,323·09 km/h).

The F-100 was to give valuable service during the early stages of the Vietnam War, and continues in service with a number of NATO nations.

Once called the 'missile with a man in it', the Lockheed F-104 Starfighter certainly provides breathtaking performance. Its initial rate of climb is 40,000 ft (12,192 m) a minute, representing about 450 mph (724 km/h) —upwards!

Its needle-nosed fuselage wrapped tightly around a powerful turbojet engine is illustrated clearly in the picture (69). The extremely small-span wing can be seen to advantage in the illustration of what is presumably the last production version, the F104S (70), construction of 205 for the Italian Air Force being scheduled to end during 1976.

The Starfighter arms many NATO nations, and its 20-mm Vulcan gun and ability to deploy two or four Sidewinder air-to-air missiles make it a formidable adversary.

70

Contemporary with Lockheed's Starfighter was the English Electric, later British Aircraft Corporation (BAC) Lightning (71), designed by W. E. W. Petter who was responsible also for the design of Britain's first jet-bomber, the English Electric Canberra.

It was a significant aircraft for the RAF—its first single-seat fighter able to exceed the speed of sound in level flight. Not only is it capable of flight at Mach 2, with a ceiling of 60,000 ft (18,290 m), but it is also what is known as an integrated weapons system.

This means that once its search radar has located the target it can be 'locked-on', feeding information to an on-board computer which provides steering information. When the Lightning is within missile-firing range, the homing heads of the missiles also 'lock-on', and the pilot is then instructed to fire his weapons. This action can be taken to destroy a target without it ever being seen by the pilot, except as a 'blip' on a radar screen.

We have seen already that when designers wanted to create an aircraft which could be flown faster than the speed of sound, one of the primary requirements was a swept wing of special aerofoil section.

Clearly, this is a specialized wing configuration which is most efficient in high-speed flight and, consequently, not ideal for the slow speeds associated with the critical manoeuvres of take-off and landing. For those flight regimes an unswept wing of 'fat' aerofoil section generates more lift.

Designers concluded that a wing which was unswept for take-off and landing, and which could be changed to a swept position for high-speed flight, would be a valuable compromise. Tests showed this

7

7

to be true, and a number of aircraft have been developed with variable-geometry wings, more commonly known as 'swing wings'.

In America, General Dynamics evolved the world's first operational fighter to have variable wing sweepback, this receiving the designation F-111 (72). Since this aircraft's introduction into service, both tactical fighter and strategic bomber versions have been developed.

F-111As of the USAF's Tactical Air Force wings saw operational service in the closing stages of the Vietnam war, not only proving to be highly effective, but recording also the lowest loss rate of any USAF aircraft deployed in Southeast Asia.

If World War II had demonstrated effectively that battleships were sitting ducks when air power was deployed effectively, it had shown also that the aircraft carrier was a very important weapon of war. As a result, the US began to build up a large carrier fleet. The wartime development of turbine engines and nuclear weapons meant that comparatively small aircraft would be able to operate from such vessels, and yet pack a punch that would have needed an entire squadron of heavy bombers in 1939.

In 1949 the Douglas Aircraft Company completed a design study for a carrier-based attack bomber known as the Skywarrior (73), which received the designation A3D, changed subsequently to A-3. When it entered service in March 1956 it was the largest aircraft produced for carrier operation, with a wing span of 72 ft 6 in (22·07 m) and a gross weight of 73,000 lb (33,112 kg).

When used operationally, however, during the Vietnam War, the Skywarrior's primary utilization was as a carrier-based electronic reconnaissance aircraft.

74

Experience had shown also that one of the most valuable categories of aircraft were those able to fulfil close-support and interdiction roles. The Korean War had proved that when aircraft were in operation on the other side of the world, an aircraft carrier provided an ideal operational base, with most facilities of a land airfield. These two reasons explain why the US Navy drew up the specification for just such an aircraft to equip Navy and Marine attack squadrons.

Douglas met the requirement by a comparatively simple low-cost lightweight aircraft, providing the Navy with one that was almost half the weight of that contemplated in the original specification.

The first of these A-4 Skyhawks (74) were manufactured by Douglas and entered service in 1956: the later company of McDonnell Douglas— formed by a merger in 1967—were still building new advanced-version A-4s in 1974.

A single-seater with a maximum level speed of 675 mph (1,086 km/h) and the ability to carry up to 10,000 lb (4,535 kg) of assorted weapons on external strong points, the A-4 proved to be of primary importance during the Vietnam War.

While Douglas was busy with the Navy's Skyhawk, the McDonnell Aircraft Corporation began development of a high-performance attack two-seater, also for the US Navy. During the development period the specification was changed, requiring provision of air-to-air armament, and leading to a versatile multi-mission two-seater able to operate as a land- and carrier-based fighter/ fighter-bomber.

Known as the F-4 Phantom II, it entered service with the Navy in December 1960, and trials for suitability in a ground-attack role led to USAF versions which entered service in 1963. Armament of the Phantom includes Sparrow and Sidewinder missiles, with the ability to carry a total of 16,000 lb (7,250 kg) of mixed weapons.

Readily identified by the dihedral on the outer wing panels and the sharp anhedral of the tailplane, Phantoms serve also with the RAF, the Luftwaffe, and the air forces of Iran, South Korea, Israel, Japan, Turkey, Greece and Spain.

Illustrated is a Luftwaffe RF-4E (75), a reconnaissance fighter version. It is a photograph which demonstrates clearly how effective a good camouflage scheme can be.

75

Chance Vought Inc were winners of a design competition to provide the US Navy with a carrier-based supersonic fighter. Clearly, such a category of aircraft was a designer's nightmare, for the kind of wing that was needed for the low approach speeds of deck landings seemed unlikely to be suitable for supersonic flight. The solution was novel: a two-position variable-incidence wing that gave good controllability at low speeds.

Designated as the F-8 Crusader, the first F-8As began to enter service in March 1957. Most-built version was the F-8E, which had armament comprising four 20 mm cannon and carried four Sidewinder missiles. Late production F-8Es had underwing pylons for the carriage of a wide range of attack weapons.

A total of 42 F-8E(FN)s were supplied also to the French Navy for service on the carriers **Clemenceau** and **Foch**, and these had additional aero-dynamic modifications to the wings to permit them to operate from these smaller vessels.

The large incidence of the wing for take-off and landing is seen clearly in the illustration of an F-8E **(76)**, while the in-flight photograph of the F-8J **(77)** shows the incidence of the wing in flight.

It is interesting to note that most of the American attack aircraft evolved in the 1955–65 period were for Navy or Marine use, underlining the continuation of the 'floating aerodrome' policy.

In 1964 Ling-Temco-Vought (LTV), resulting from the merger of Vought with Ling-Temco Electronics, were the winners of a US Navy competition for the design of a new lightweight attack aircraft. One requirement was that initial production aircraft had to be in service by 1967, and LTV gained by basing the new design on the successful F-8, which promised speedier production and cost savings.

No longer requiring supersonic capability it was possible to dispense with the variable-incidence wing, and fuselage length was reduced also. Designated A-7 Corsair II, the first A-7As (78) were delivered to squadrons in October 1966 and were in operation in Vietnam in 1967.

Evaluation of the Corsair prior to its introduction into Naval squadron service had shown the potential of the design, and in October 1966 the USAF ordered A-7D Corsairs (79), this illustration giving an excellent appreciation of the external armament carried by modern attack aircraft.

80
81

Successful testing of the Gloster-Whittle E.28/39 at RAF Cranwell in 1941 had left no doubt that new and excitingly powerful turbine engines would be developed eventually. When America was advised of the new power plant, the General Electric Company began to build engines based on the Whittle design, subsequently developing and initiating original design.

As we have already seen, the new engines had been utilized to power a whole new generation of fighter aircraft, the very first of which had been Bell's P-59 Airacomet, which flew for the first time on 1 October 1942.

One project which started a few months after the first flight of the P-59 was the design and production of the first swept-wing jet bomber to be produced in quantity for any air force. This was the Boeing B-47 Stratojet (80), powered by six underwing turbojets. So thin and flexible were the wings of this revolutionary medium bomber that, when the aircraft was on the ground, they drooped to give an appearance of anhedral. When loaded and in flight, however, they were seen to be set at a conventional dihedral angle. This flexible wing was strong enough for the Stratojet to use a low-level 'lob-bombing' technique, with the bomb being released during a zooming vertical climb, and the aircraft disengaging by completing a fighter tactic, the Immelmann turn.

Friction between the Eastern and Western powers had been greatly intensified during the period of the Berlin Airlift, an operation which cost valuable lives and a great deal of money. It served only to prove to the Soviet Union that the Western Allies were prepared to face grave problems or any cost if it would maintain peace. Two years later came the next major confrontation, with the beginning of war in Korea in mid-1950. The question in most minds then was: can this escalate into the third world war?

Undoubtedly it could have done, but by that time Russia had already demonstrated an ability to deploy atomic weapons. Thus came about the nuclear deterrent policy, with both East and West capable of annihilating attack. So unthinkable is an all-out nuclear war that, to this day, the deterrent threat has proved adequate to prevent a major conflict.

One of the keystones of America's deterrent policy was to be the Boeing B-52 Stratofortress (81). This strategic heavy bomber, with a wing span of 185 ft (56·39 m) and powered by eight turbojet or turbofan engines, was capable of delivering nuclear weapons on any target in the world. Their value was proven in 1962 when Soviet missile sites were discovered on Cuba. Faced with a full-scale nuclear alert, a percentage of Strategic Air Command's B-52's were kept airborne around the clock. When opposed by such determination, the Russians dismantled the sites and shipped the missiles back East.

83

Preceding page:
To enable aircraft like the B-52 to
remain airborne for long periods it is
necessary for them to take on additional
supplies of fuel while in flight. This
technique of flight-refuelling had
originated from quite early days, the US
Army Air Service pioneering the idea
in 1923.

When three B-52 Stratofortresses
completed a 45 hour 19 minute round-
the-world flight in 1957, they had been
refuelled en route three times by KC-97
tankers. These tanker aircraft had been
developed from the Boeing-built C-97
Stratofreighter and at a later date the
Boeing C-135 turbojet-powered Strato-
lifter also became available as the
KC-135 Stratotanker.

At the opposite end of the scale,
aircraft like the Douglas A-3 Skywarrior
have also been modified to serve as
tankers, able to supply range-extending
fuel to fast fighters, while other suitable
aircraft have been converted to provide
helicopters with the facility of an airborne
filling station.

The US services make considerable use
of a 'Flying-Boom' refuelling system,
developed by Boeing, which is controlled
by an operator who 'flies' the boom into a
suitable position for the receiving aircraft
to connect with it. The illustration shows
an F-4E **(82)** approaching the 'Flying-
Boom'.

An Air Ministry specification was drawn
up in 1948 to equip the RAF with a
force of long-range medium jet-bombers
which, armed with conventional or
nuclear weapons, would provide a
modern striking force.

Known as the 'V' bomber programme,
it initiated production of the Vickers
Valiant—withdrawn from service in 1965;
the Avro Vulcan; and Handley Page
Victor. B.1 versions of this latter aircraft
were delivered to the first operational
squadrons in April 1958, and when
superseded by Victor B.2s were converted to flight-refuelling tankers.

In Britain a different technique of
flight-refuelling has developed, known as
the drogue and probe method. The tanker
trails a hose with a conical drogue at its
end. Into this the thirsty aircraft pushes a
rigid probe, an automatic valve then

effecting a fuel-tight seal.

The illustration **(83)** shows a Victor tanker using the probe and drogue system to suckle an RAF Buccaneer low-level strike aircraft.

This page:

A small nation seeking a particular class of aircraft has to evaluate whether it can be built or bought most cheaply. The former decision applies usually only when large numbers are involved, or there are prospects of sales to other nations.

The vast productive capacity of the American aircraft industry has made it possible for them to build new aeroplanes at comparatively low prices, and as a result this country has sold large numbers of aircraft to a worldwide market in the years since World War II.

When Spain was needing a general-

purpose amphibian for patrol and rescue duties, the requirement was met by buying a supply from Grumman Aircraft in America. This company had designed and built such an aircraft for the US Navy, known as the Albatross.

The illustration **(84)** shows a line-up of these aircraft in Spanish service, in which they have the designation AN-1 Albatross.

When a moderate number of aircraft are required, an alternative means of procuring them is by licence production. By payment of a licence fee, the designing company passes on the drawings and know-how, enabling the foreign company to build the requisite number of aircraft without having to face any unknowns or astronomical develop-ment costs.

The Northrop Corporation in America had designed a relatively simple light-weight fighter to US Government requirements for supply to friendly nations under the Military Assistance Program (MAP). Spain elected to manufacture her own version of Northrop's F-5, and Construcciones Aeronautica SA (CASA) was contracted by the Spanish Air Force to construct, under licence, 36 single-seat fighters and 34 two-seat fighter/trainers, these having the respective Spanish designa-tions of C.9 and CE.9. Built by CASA's factories at Getafe and Seville, the first ten entered service in June 1969.

Illustrated is a reconnaissance version developed by Northrop as the RF-5A, and built in Spain under the designation CR.9 **(85)**. Ports in the nose are for the four installed reconnaissance cameras.

The adjoining country of France, however, has a flourishing and forward-looking aircraft industry of its own which, in the years since the end of World War II, has produced some remarkable aircraft.

Avions Marcel Dassault (now known as Dassault/Breguet Aviation following a merger with the pioneering company of Breguet, founded by Louis Breguet in 1911) was responsible for design of the Mirage delta-wing all-weather high-altitude intercepter, of which the prototype first flew on 17 November 1957.

The delta-wing configuration was chosen because it not only provides a very rigid and enduring airframe structure, capable of supersonic flight, but the large wing area provides excellent performance and handling at high altitude.

Since that time a whole family of Mirage aircraft have been developed. The Mirage 5 ground-attack version, which flew for the first time on 19 May 1967, retains the delta-wing configuration of the parent Mirage. Illustrated is the Mirage 5V **(86)** being built for Venezuela.

Although the Mirage was established as a successful design, Dassault began the private-venture development of a new single-seat multi-mission fighter in the mid-1960s.

Designated as the Mirage F1, it differs from the basic family likeness by dispensing with the delta-wing configuration in favour of a swept wing and conventional all-moving tailplane. Advanced aerodynamic features of this wing enable the F1 to take off on an interception sortie in only 2,100 ft (640 m), even when

88

86

87

operating from unprepared strips.

It is a formidable aeroplane, armed with two 30 mm cannon, able to deploy Sidewinder missiles, to carry up to 8,820 lb (4,000 kg) of weapons externally, and to fly at Mach 2·2 (approx 1,460 mph: 2,350 km/h at 40,000 ft: 12,000 m). Illustration (87) shows the Dassault/Breguet production line of F1s.

In Britain, the delta-wing configuration chosen by Dassault for the Mirage was used by A. V. Roe and Company when they designed their contribution to the RAF's 'V' bomber programme.

This wing configuration was chosen by Avro for the same characteristic which had appealed to the French manufacturer. In addition, its use for a large bomber aircraft meant that the depth of the wing section would be adequate to contain fuel and bomb-load without any external drag.

The Avro Vulcan (88) flew for the first time on 30 August 1952, entering service in mid-1956, and despite a subsonic speed was regarded as one of the world's most redoubtable bomber aircraft. Confirmation of the excellence of the structural design is given by the fact that

Vulcans were still in RAF service in 1974, and there was talk of converting some aircraft for a strategic reconnaissance role.

Following page:
Supermarine, builders of the S.6B seaplane and Spitfire fighter, were to evolve a new interceptor for the RAF in the post-war years. Instead of the delta-wing chosen by Dassault for the Mirage III at a slightly later date, Supermarine elected to use the swept wing and conventional tailplane, to which the French manufacturers reverted. The resulting aircraft, the Supermarine Swift F.1, entered service with the RAF in 1952, but proving unsuitable as an interceptor only 36 aircraft (F.1s and F.2s combined) were built.

Developed from the interceptor was the Swift F.R.5 (89), a fighter-reconnaissance aircraft which was to see five years of service with the RAF before being replaced by the Hawker Hunter F.R.10 in 1961. In the F.R.5 Swift an extended nose carried three cameras, and armament comprised two 30 mm Aden guns, with provisions for bombs or rockets which were carried on underwing hard points.

One of the great technological achievements of World War II was radar. Intended originally for the detection and location of enemy aircraft, as it became developed it was to prove also a remarkable device for accurate navigation, the interception of enemy aircraft by night, and the blind bombing of ground targets.

It was discovered, however, that under certain circumstances it was possible for low-flying aircraft to escape detection. To exploit this weakness in an enemy's defences, the British Admiralty sought a carrier-based low-level strike aircraft. Blackburn Aircraft were chosen to build this aeroplane, the prototype of which flew for the first time on 30 April 1958.

Ten years later, the type was chosen by the RAF to close the gap in its ranks caused by the vacillations of successive governments, resulting in the Hawker Siddeley Buccaneer (90).

The type continues in RAF service, a significant strike aircraft which uses terrain-following techniques for low-level attack, and which is able to deliver nuclear or conventional bombs and rockets, as well as Bullpup or Martel missiles.

91

92

In the scramble for military superiority which has been taking place between East and West since the end of World War II, there have been many changes of ideas as new weapons and counter-weapons evolved. The ICBM was once considered the ultimate weapon, but it was realized that once their fixed launch sites had been identified, they became primary and vulnerable targets for a well-informed enemy. Hence the American B-52 and British Vulcan, both able to deploy nuclear stand-off bombs, providing a mobile rather than static launch site for these weapons. Unfortunately, aircraft need aerodromes, which can be put out of commission and, even when airborne, can still be spotted, intercepted and destroyed.

So has developed the nuclear submarine which, invisible beneath the sea, can launch ballistic missiles without surfacing. Their detection and destruction poses a very different problem.

Among the anti-submarine patrol bombers developed to meet this threat is the Lockheed P-3 Orion (91). Carrying magnetic anomaly detection (MAD) equipment and sono-buoys to locate underwater craft, it can be armed with nuclear depth bombs, torpedoes, mines and rockets to deal with the enemy vessel when its position has been ascertained.

France has also developed an effective maritime patrol aircraft to fulfil the same task as the P-3 Orion. This is the Breguet Br.1150 Atlantic (92), selected from 25 submissions in response to a NATO design competition.

Built by a consortium of European manufacturers, under the overall leadership of Breguet, it is in production for use by the navies of France, Germany, Italy and the Netherlands. Like the Orion it has MAD equipment, but has also a tail-fin pod containing electronic counter-measures (ECM) and a retractable radar 'dustbin' beneath the forward fuselage.

The internal weapons bay of the Atlantic can accommodate all standard NATO bombs, depth charges and homing torpedoes. The illustration shows clearly the radar 'dustbin', and gives some idea of the capacity of the bomb bay.

Britain, too, has an important long-range maritime patrol aircraft, the first turbofan-powered anti-submarine aircraft to be built anywhere in the world.

This is the Hawker Siddeley Nimrod, which has been developed from the Comet 4C airliner, and the first of these was delivered to Strike Command's No. 201 Squadron at Kinloss on 2 October 1969.

Like the Atlantic it has MAD and ECM, plus sono-buoys and an Autolycus ionization detector to 'sniff out' any shipping below. It carries also a search-light for night attack and advanced air-to-surface radar. It can use depth charges, mines, bombs and torpedoes to attack the enemy, as well as Aérospatiale's AS.12 air-to-surface wire-guided missiles, which are carried beneath the wing.

The illustration (93) shows an RAF Nimrod which has located and is circling to inspect a Russian submarine.

Remote from the horrors of warfare, and the implied threat of destruction posed by the nuclear-powered submarines, it is refreshing to find that not all of the aviation scene is concerned with war.

This delightful view, from the other side of the world, shows the fleet of light aircraft operated by New Zealand's Southern Scenic Airways (94).

They are employed primarily to convey tourists to out of the way beauty spots, so that even if it is their one and only visit to that delightful country they will remember, forever, not only the beauty and peace, but these wonderfully safe lightweight aircraft which carry out such pleasant duties all over the world.

Strangely, pilots of aircraft often have an affinity for water. Perhaps this is because the systems of navigation evolved by our seagoing forebears have proved invaluable to the airborne fraternity. Despite the development of sophisticated navigational systems, it is good to be able to use the basic methods of 'finding your way', for even the most advanced electronics can go on strike.

Be that as it may, many light aircraft, such as this Rollason-built Druine D.31 Turbulent (95) which was designed as a landplane, have been converted to operate on floats. There is a fascination all its own in landing and taking off from water, heightened especially when its venue is some remote or secret stretch of lake that can be reached only by such craft as these.

95

Another aspect of aviation is covered also by lightweight aircraft, for many aeroplanes in this category provide much of the fun and excitement still to be enjoyed by participating in, or merely being a spectator at, one of the many air shows. In Britain, which is not renowned for the reliability and duration of its summer, the calendar still seems to be crowded with aviation events.

So popular, indeed, have air shows become that aerobatic teams, like that once sponsored by the Rothman Tobacco Company, were often booked a good year ahead, for the precision and skill of their display was a real crowd-puller.

The illustration (96) shows the team flying its Stampe SV-4Cs, used with distinction before the acquisition of their squad of Pitts S-2A Specials.

96

97

The Pitts aircraft flown by the Rothman team originate from the drawing-board of Mr Curtis Pitts, one of the best-known US designers of high-performance sporting aircraft. His original single-seat Pitts Special was designed in 1943–44, and many examples have been constructed by devotees of the homebuilding movement which is very active in America.

Such factors as good weather and, in the past, cheap and plentiful petrol, have contributed to the growth of this movement, aided considerably by the Experimental Aircraft Association (EAA) which gives help and advice to amateur constructors.

Typical of the very basic craft designed for and built by these enthusiasts is the RLU Breezy (97), which was designed by three professional pilots. More than 350 sets of construction plans had been sold by early 1976, with examples being built in Australia, Canada and South Africa, as well as in its homeland.

More professional in appearance, and of course more difficult to build, is the Bede BD-4 **(98)**.

Designed especially for the home-builder by Mr James R. Bede, that illustrated shows the extremely high standard of product quality achieved by enthusiastic amateurs. It is for these real enthusiasts that men like Jim Bede have devoted untold hours of work. Their aim has been to simplify methods of construction so that builders of quite moderate skill can create aircraft of which they can be proud, and which they can fly easily and safely.

Even more advanced in the US home-built category are those aircraft which are built to participate in the very popular National Air Races.

Illustrated is a Knight Twister Imperial **(99)**, intended for air racing in the Sports Biplane class, and which was built by Mr Don Fairbanks of Cincinnati, Ohio. The plans for this little aeroplane, which has a wingspan of only 17 ft 6 in (5·33 m), were specially modified from the standard Knight Twister. Designed by Mr Vernon Payne, kits of parts are also available to help simplify the task for the 'do-it-yourself' plane builder.

And when completed, even the standard Knight Twister can provide a maximum 160 mph (257 km/h) from a 90 hp engine.

Still in the lightplane class there is, of course, a wide variety of one to six-seat aircraft of superb quality manufactured by companies all over the world who cater for the private pilot who wishes to buy his aircraft ready-made.

In America there are a host of manufacturers, headed by the 'big three' of Beech, Cessna and Piper, whose aircraft are not only a pleasure to see, but a delight to fly, or be flown in.

The illustration **(100)** shows production lines at the Beech factory in Wichita, Kansas. The foreground is dominated by a line of Barons, many of which have entered USAF service, serving to remind us that even light aircraft have military potential.

For example, the Beech T-34 Mentor **(101)**, which derived from the basic Beech Model 35 Bonanza, was selected first by the USAF as a primary trainer.

Both the US Army and Navy were to buy substantial quantities of these aircraft, and they were built in Canada for the USAF and RCAF, in Japan for the JASDF and Philippine Air Force, and at Cordoba in the Argentine.

The aircraft illustrated carries a Mexican registration, and these trainers have been supplied also to Chile, Colombia, El Salvador, Saudi Arabia, Spain, Turkey and Venezuela.

102

A fairly recent entrant into the American lightplane market is Grumman, who in late 1972 merged with American Aviation Corporation, thereby gaining a product line of lightplanes, which are marketed under the name Grumman American Aviation Corporation. And in West Germany the company of Rhein-Flugzeugbau (RFB) also became interested in the same market, acquiring a 50 per cent holding in the German lightplane company Sportavia-Pützer.

In April 1974 these American and German companies announced they had jointly developed an unusual lightplane powered by a Wankel-type engine driving a ducted-fan system evolved by RFB. Known as the Fanliner **(102)**, it utilizes the adhesive-bonding technique of airframe construction, as well as many components of the Grumman American Trainer and Traveler. It demonstrates, very well, that new ideas still abound in the aviation world.

101

Special Aircraft

New applications are evolving constantly, and these have given rise to specialized aircraft which provide an important contribution to modern life. Typical are the agricultural aircraft in widespread use throughout the world, spreading fertilizers and crop spraying or crop dusting.

These are, indeed, specialized aircraft, such as the Quail Commander (103) built in Mexico. This was designed originally by the Rockwell Standard Corporation, with careful attention to safety features, for it is no easy and safe task following the contours of hilly terrain at low level. Hence there are provided wire cutters, in case of collision with hard-to-see telephone cables, rugged seats and safety harness, well padded cockpit interiors and tough tubular steel structures to maintain the integrity of the cockpit area in a crash.

And, of course, they need also hoppers for chemicals or liquid, fan or engine-driven spray booms, medium and high volume spreader systems, and even floodlights for night operations: specialized indeed.

An unusual category of special aircraft is the water-bomber, the Canadair CL-215 (104) being designed and developed in Canada to deal with the problem of controlling large-scale forest fires.

There is, of course, nothing like water for damping the enthusiasm of even the most spirited fire, and the CL-215 is designed to uplift 1,200 Imp gallons (5,455 litres) of water which can be dropped in one vast all-enveloping mass. Water plus chemical retardants can be loaded before take-off, or the water bomber can scoop up its own supply in 16–20 seconds while skimming the surface of a lake, river or the sea. One CL-215 operated in France by the Protection Civile dropped a total of 98,397 Imp gallons (447,309 litres) of water in a single day during the summer of 1970, representing a weight of almost 432 tons!

103

104

105

But perhaps the most strange aircraft of today are the remotely piloted vehicles (RPVs), pilotless high-performance aircraft which are designed for a specific role. They have already proved themselves in the violence of war, for reconnaissance RPVs not only brought back superb pictures of enemy positions and defences in Vietnam, but achieved this without putting a human pilot at risk.

The Lockheed Hercules has already been mentioned as an RPV carrier, and here we see the scene beneath the wing of one of these big transports (105), which shows a Teledyne Ryan Model 234 RPV (BGM-34A) mounted on its launch pylon. It is a case very similar to that posed by the well known verse: 'Big fleas have little fleas upon their backs to bite 'em; little fleas have lesser fleas, and so **ad infinitum**,' for you will see that the RPV is itself being given a payload beneath its wing.

In fact, the load carried by the RPV is a HOBOS (HOming BOmb System) developed by Rockwell International. This is, in effect, a modular kit which is used to convert a conventional general-purpose bomb into a homing bomb.

When launched from the RPV by remote command, the guidance section of the nose of HOBOS seeks the target, locks on to it, and is guided by its own autopilot to the point of impact.

The illustration (106) shows the Hercules climbing away on a mission, an RPV beneath the starboard wing, and the RPV itself carrying two weapons beneath its wings.

When it is still many miles from the target the Hercules is able to launch and control the RPV, which is in itself a complex mini-aircraft, although one must not be confused by that word mini.

The Ryan Model 234, for example, has a wing span of 14 ft 6 in (4·42 m), length overall of 23 ft 7¼ in (7·19 m) and a launch weight of 2,800 lb (1,270 kg). Its power plant consists of a 1,700 lb (771 kg) thrust turbojet engine, and while its maximum speed is secret information, it is known that many RPVs are capable of performance in the Mach 1 to Mach 1·8 range.

Not surprisingly, it is a difficult target to intercept by any means, their weapons scoring an even higher percentage of direct hits (107).

06

07

We must not overlook the other main category of aircraft, once considered to be little more than inventors' follies—the helicopter.

Wood and metal propeller toys had given convincing proof that a rotary wing could climb straight up into the air. It even worked to some extent for experimental aircraft, but as soon as there was any forward motion of the vehicle it would overturn and crash.

It took many years to appreciate why this happened. Once understood it was ridiculously simple. The blade advancing into the airstream caused by the aircraft's forward motion, developed more lift than the opposite retreating blade. It was not until 1923 that the Spaniard, Juan de la Cierva, invented an ingenious flapping hinge for each blade which made the rotary wing a practical proposition. Roughly twenty years later Igor Sikorsky flew the world's first practical single-rotor helicopter, and a whole new category of heavier-than-air craft became reality.

One of the earliest helicopters in British military service was the two-seat Saro Skeeter (108) which, powered by a 200 hp engine, was able to record a maximum speed of about 100 mph (160 km/h).

First British-designed helicopter to enter service with the RAF was the Sycamore, developed by the Bristol Aeroplane Company. Very similar in appearance to the Saro Skeeter it was, however, considerably bigger and could accommodate a crew of two or three passengers. Powered by a 550 hp Alvis Leonides engine, the Sycamore had a maximum speed of 127 mph (204 km/h) at sea level but, like most early helicopters, had a somewhat restricted range.

Nevertheless, it was to prove an important aircraft for the RAF, for with it they discovered and developed new techniques that were to become inseparable from the role of the helicopter: rescue and pick-up by power-driven hoist; and the ability to put down or pick up troops in areas inaccessible to any other form of transport.

The Royal Navy were also to use a small number of Sycamores (109) for experimental purposes.

As a result of their experiments the Royal Navy was convinced, very quickly, that the helicopter could prove to be an important naval auxiliary.

Its ability to hover or match its speed to that of a surface vessel was particularly exciting, not only for tasks such as rescue patrol alongside aircraft carriers, but because it suggested the possibility of even very small ships being able to carry an aircraft. If this was feasible, then ship-to-shore and ship-to-ship communications would be greatly improved, and a ship's commander would have his eyes extended far beyond the normal limit of the horizon.

Time was not only to prove these premises to be true, but to show that much more could be achieved by a vessel with its own attendant helicopter.

The Westland Wasp (110) was the Navy's first helicopter to operate extensively from platforms on frigates and smaller vessels. It was soon discovered that they could not only fulfil such tasks as those mentioned above but that, small though they were, they could deploy torpedoes and air-to-surface missiles.

11

Far more sophisticated is the turbine-powered Westland Wessex, serving both the Royal Navy and Royal Air Force.

A development of the piston-engined Sikorsky S-58, this British-built helicopter has been given the benefits of turbine power, the first production version having the designation H.A.S.Mk 1, and entering service with the Navy in 1960. The RAF's version is the H.C.Mk 2, which differs in its power plant, comprising two coupled-shaft turbines, replacing the single larger turbine in the Naval version.

The RAF Wessex illustrated (111) can carry up to 16 troops, be used as an air ambulance with seven litters, transport up to 4,000 lb (1,814 kg) of cargo, and has provision for the fitment of machine-guns and rocket-launchers.

Westland Helicopters at Yeovil, Somerset, has a close technical association with Sikorsky Aircraft in America. The link stretches back for more than a quarter of a century, for the company's first helicopter was built in 1947 after acquisition of a licence to build

the Sikorsky S-51, which it produced as the Westland Dragonfly.

A more recent and closer tie has been developed with Aérospatiale in France for, under the Anglo-French helicopter agreement of 1967, the two companies have worked together to design and develop some important new helicopters.

One of these is the Aérospatiale/Westland SA341 Gazelle which is in production in France for the French Army, military export and civil use, and by Westland for the British Army, Navy and Air Force. Illustrated (112) is the civil version, which offers luxurious high-speed transport for a pilot and up to four passengers.

Igor Sikorsky was the pioneer of the helicopter in the US, and the company which he founded in 1923 was to lead the world in helicopter production for some time.

Since then other manufacturers have come along with new ideas and designs to challenge that lead, including Bell, Boeing-Vertol, Kaman and Lockheed.

Bell's Model 47 achieved the distinction of receiving from the US Civil Aviation Authority the first helicopter Approved Type Certificate in 1946, and was to remain in production for 25 years. This remarkable, but very basic, three-seat helicopter is a far cry from Bell's Long Ranger (113) first announced in late 1973. A general-purpose civil helicopter, it has standard accommodation for a crew of two and four passengers. First production aircraft were delivered in late 1975.

It introduces a remarkable break-through in the long-term search for a means to eliminate the vibration associated with all rotary-winged aircraft. Named the 'Noda-Matic' system, it utilizes the long-known scientific fact that a beam subjected to vertical vibration develops flexing in a wave form. In such a beam nodal points, equidistant from the centre, have no relative motion, and Bell have used the nodal points of a beam to connect fuselage and rotor system so providing an exceedingly smooth helicopter ride.

12

13

Helicopters introduced into the Korean War showed immediately that rotary-winged aircraft were to be a most valuable addition to the equipment of the fighting services. Not only were they able to put down and pick up troops in areas where no other vehicle could go, but their speedy evacuation of front-line casualties was to reduce the incidence of death from wounds to the lowest recorded in military history.

It was discovered very soon, however, that at the moment when a 'chopper' was dropping or picking up men or cargo, it was extremely vulnerable to enemy attack. Weapons were required to provide a hail of fire and force the enemy to 'keep their heads down' until the no-movement period of maximum vulnerability had passed. Highly effective gunship helicopters have evolved from this small beginning, and their deployment in Vietnam showed them to be a valuable close-support weapon.

Bell developed the Model 209 Huey-Cobra **(114)**, a turbine-powered armed helicopter with various armament installations, which include Miniguns and/or grenade-launchers in a chin turret, and folding-fin rockets, cannon or Minigun pods carried beneath stub-wings. Progressive development of the type has meant that Bell is one of two manufacturers who in 1975 were building prototypes of a potent Advanced Attack Helicopter (AAH) for the US Army.

The prototype of Bell's AAH has the designation YAH-63, and its family likeness to the HueyCobra can be seen in the accompanying illustration **(115)**. It is, however, a very different aircraft, with two 1,500 shp advanced technology turboshaft engines replacing the single 1,800 shp turboshaft of the Huey, a large ventral fin with a horizontal surface mounted at the tip of the upper fin, and a very advanced dynamic system which includes rotor blades with dual stainless steel spars to improve combat survivability.

Primary task of the AAH is the destruction of enemy armour, which means they will be equipped with 'tank-busting' weapons. Those of the Bell AAH include a three-barrel 30 mm gun in an under-nose turret, 2·75 in folding-fin rockets or TOW anti-tank missiles beneath the stub wings, with a stabilized telescopic sight to guide the missiles by day and an infra-red vision system for use by night.

115

114

117

118

In a much heavier class is the Boeing Vertol CH-47 Chinook (116), a twin-engine twin-rotor medium transport helicopter that entered service with the US Army in late 1962.

The illustration shows typical battle-field usage of the type, lifting a field gun and its ammunition to a forward position, the gun crew with additional ammunition and supplies accommodated within the helicopter's cabin.

Cabin accommodation will cater for a maximum of 44 troops, or 24 litters and two medical attendants for casualty evacuation from front-line positions. Alternatively, the Chinook can be used for all-cargo missions, when the latest CH-47C has a maximum internal payload of 18,600 lb (8,437 kg) or an external cargo capability of 23,212 lb (10, 528 kg).

These aircraft proved especially valuable in Vietnam for the retrieval of crashed aircraft, and during their use in this theatre of operations they were

responsible for recovering at least 11,500 aircraft that were worth well over $3·0 billion.

In the Soviet Union the development of rotary-winged aircraft has gone ahead for the same reasons as in the West, but it would appear that large passenger-carrying helicopters have been produced in far greater quantities. The Mil Mi-6, when first announced in 1957, was then the largest helicopter flying anywhere in the world. Powered by two large turbo-shaft engines to drive its single 114 ft 10 in (35·00 m) main rotor, it has accommodation for 65 passengers.

Somewhat smaller is the Mil Mi-8 (117), that illustrated being in Aeroflot service and equipped to carry up to 32 passengers. Following large-scale use of gunships by US forces involved in Vietnam, Russia has become interested in this class of helicopter. The Mi-8 has been used for picking up and putting down

troops during army exercises, and it is believed that outriggers on the landing gear have been used to mount a variety of weapons.

In a totally different class to the Mi-8 however, is Mil's Mi-12 (118) four-engined twin-rotor heavy duty helicopter which holds a string of records for pay-loads lifted to various height levels.

The four Soloviev turboshaft engines that power this Soviet giant have a combined output of 26,000 shp for take-off, enabling the Mi-12 to become airborne at a maximum gross weight of 231,500 lb (105,000 kg), and to carry a payload of 78,000 lb (35,400 kg) for a distance of 310 miles (500 km).

The unusual layout for the twin rotors, namely side by side above the tips of fixed-wings, was chosen because it is believed to offer better stability and longer life than the more conventional tandem layout as used for the Chinook.

Current Military & Civil Aircraft

With our emphasis being on military aircraft, it is worth taking a final look around at some of the advanced aircraft in use with the world's air forces, or which are being developed as new-generation aircraft.

It will be recalled that Northrop in the US had developed a lightweight tactical fighter designated F-5, which was supplied to Allied nations under MAP. When the US Government initiated a design competition to acquire a new International Fighter Aircraft (IFA) to succeed the F-5, Northrop proposed an advanced version of the same aircraft, and in November 1970 it was announced that this company had won the competition.

Their resulting F-5E Tiger II **(119)** has more powerful turbojet engines, advanced electronics and equipment, and is able to deploy an amazingly wide variety of weapons from underfuselage and underwing hard points, which can accommodate a total of 7,000 lb (3,157 kg). Maximum level speed is Mach 1·6, slightly faster than the F-5, but manoeuvrability rather than speed is considered the most important feature of this new aircraft, which has leading-edge manoeuvring flaps similar to those developed for the Royal Netherlands Air Force's NF-5A/Bs.

It came as no great surprise when Grumman Corporation were announced the winner of a design competition to provide a new carrier-based multi-role fighter for the US Navy, for this company, has a long tradition of building naval and maritime aircraft.

Required to be fast—it has a maximum design speed of Mach 2·34—the F-14 Tomcat **(120)** has variable-geometry wings to allow the slow approach speeds required for all-weather deck landings.

Armament will consist initially of four Sparrow air-to-air missiles, carried partially buried in the fuselage, plus various combinations of other weapons to a maximum external load of 14,500 lb (6,577 kg). The second illustration **(121)** gives an excellent view of the all-important air intakes, which are so critical for high-performance aircraft, and of the small ventral fins mounted at the rear of each engine nacelle.

Towards the end of 1969, McDonnell Douglas Corporation was announced the winner of a design competition to provide the USAF with a new air superiority fighter.

There is a distinct overall similarity between this aircraft, designated as the F-15A Eagle (122), and Grumman's F-14 Tomcat. The major difference is predictable without even seeing these aircraft, for since the Eagle does not need to have the very wide speed range of the deck-landing Tomcat, it need not be involved in the complexities inseparable from a variable-geometry wing, and this is, indeed, the case.

Eagle will carry up to 12,000 lb (5,433 kg) of mixed weapons on external stations, but the really complex aspect of the weapons system is the advanced electronics, which will not only seek and acquire small high-speed targets, but will ensure that the aircraft's missiles or internal gun is fired at the right moment to ensure the target's destruction. The first aircraft to become operational was delivered to the USAF on 14 November 1974.

Visitors to Farnborough International '74 will have seen the F-15A in flight, performing its routine in appalling weather, and it is this kind of capability which must be the stock-in-trade of a successful combat fighter.

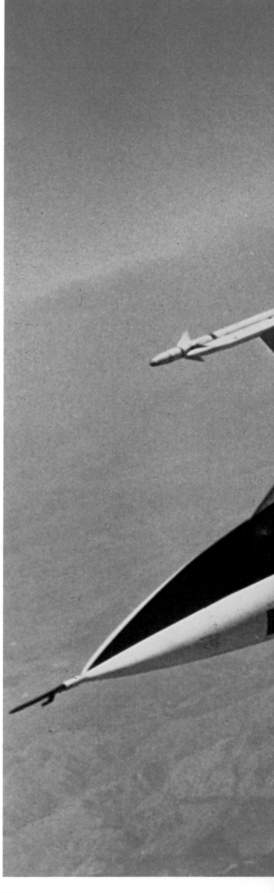

122

Five companies submitted design proposals to meet the USAF's requirement for a Lightweight Fighter Prototype, and in April 1972 General Dynamics and Northrop were selected to build competing prototypes.

This method of acquiring the most effective aeroplane for a particular role dates back to the early days of the US Army Air Service. Then it was essential to get the best machine for the job: today, when computers can predict performance

with surprising accuracy, it is not essential but desirable. Desirable because the old-fashioned rapport between man and machine—called seat-of-the-pants flying—is not so predictable. Both the contenders will almost certainly be flyable to the predicted performance. Just as certainly, one of them will be more pleasant to fly.

General Dynamics' YF-16 prototype **(123)** flew officially for the first time on 2 February 1974, competing subsequently against the Northrop YF-17 which first flew on 9 June 1974. By then the USAF had decided to evaluate these two aircraft in the role of an Air Combat Fighter (ACF), and in January 1975 the YF-16 was declared the winner. With the USAF having a requirement for up to 650 production F-16s, and with 306 more ordered by Belgium, Denmark, the Netherlands and Norway, this aircraft has become a most important weapon in the West's defence.

Though defeated in the USAF's ACF evaluation by the General Dynamics YF-16, Northrop's YF-17 remains a significant aircraft, and the 001 and 002 prototypes are seen in flight in the accompanying picture (124). The US Navy has also a requirement for an air combat fighter and initially showed considerable interest in Northrop's YF-17. However, further evaluation by the Navy showed the desirability of having a slightly-enlarged and strengthened version for service on board Fleet aircraft carriers, and a joint contract for the development of such an aircraft, under the designation F-18, was awarded to McDonnell Douglas and Northrop in May 1975. Some 8,000 lb (3,629 kg) heavier than the YF-17, and to be powered by two General Electric F404-GE-400 turbofan engines rated at about 16,000 lb (7,257 kg) static thrust,

124

12

eleven development aircraft are to be built initially.

In an age when military aircraft can travel at speeds between 1,500 and 2,000 mph (2,414 and 3,219 km/h) as routine, and when one of the major threats is that imposed by missiles, the defences need as much warning as possible of impending attack or the approach of hostile aircraft/weapons. Even when the information is received, a complex control centre is necessary to evaluate the input and initiate suitable action to contain the enemy's attack.

Obviously, the most vulnerable point of such a defence system is the control centre, for once it is put out of action it is unlikely that defensive weapons of the right kind will be launched sufficiently early.

One of the solutions to this problem lies in the provision of Airborne Warning and Control System (AWACS) aircraft. Because of their mobility in three dimensions, they are seen to offer a survivable early warning, command and control system.

Boeing have supplied the USAF with testbed aircraft, based on the 707, designated Boeing EC-137D AWACS **(125)**. The large radome, pylon-mounted from the aft fuselage, carries a 24 ft (7·32 m) diameter antenna which scans 360° around the aircraft, and from ground level up into the stratosphere. These aircraft are currently being evaluated and could prove to be an important type of aircraft for the future, with both civil and military applications.

One of the most important aircraft being procured for the USAF at the present time is the B-1 strategic bomber which has been designed and built by Rockwell International. The first of these supersonic bomber prototypes was rolled out on 26 October 1974 **(126)**.

A 'swing-wing' design, with the blended wing/body concept used for the company's submission for the F-15 fighter competition, the B-1 is designed to have a maximum speed of Mach 2·2 (approximately 1,450 mph: 2,333 km/h at 50,000 ft: 15,000 m), range of 6,100 miles (9,800 km) at its cruising speed, and the capability to uplift a maximum weapon load of 115,000 lb (52,160 kg). When it is realised that this weapon load equals the weight of nearly twenty Spitfires, one gains some appreciation of the technological advances made in military aircraft in the past 36 years.

One of the most important categories of military aircraft must always be the basic trainer. The quality and capability of an air force stems from its standard of training and the Royal Air Force has long understood this first principle. Latest trainer to be built for the RAF is the Hawker Siddeley Hawk (127), a small single-turbofan-powered tandem two-seat aircraft which is to replace the Gnat and Hunter and, ultimately, the Jet Provost.

A moderately swept wing and special trailing-edge flaps give the all-important speed range necessary, providing the essential low control speed required for a basic trainer, coupled with a maximum speed of Mach 1·13 at 48,000 ft (14,630 m), for sparkling performance as an advanced trainer. It is intended also to develop the Hawk for a close-support role, in which configuration it is designed to deploy a maximum external load of up to 5,000 lb (2,270 kg) of mixed ordnance.

The first of these aircraft to be completed flew for the first time on 21 August 1974. This was a production aircraft, which means that the Hawk will probably be unique by becoming the first military aircraft to enter service without a prototype being built and flown.

The Saab 35 Draken, which is in service with the Danish and Swedish Air Forces, is an example of specialized design to meet a specific requirement.

Swedish policy insists that in the event of a crisis her air force must not be tied slavishly to air stations, the exact position of which would be known to an enemy. Instead, they are to be dispersed throughout the country, and aircraft have to be capable of take-off from short sections of the country's main roads. This accounts for selection of the double-delta wing for the Draken, its large area allowing short take-off and landing runs.

The Saab J 35F Draken is illustrated (128), an all-weather fighter or attack aircraft, which can carry missiles, rockets and other weapons totalling 9,000 lb (4,082 kg) on external attachment points. Take-off run with nine 1,000 lb bombs is only 4,030 ft (1,210 m).

Designed to replace eventually the J 35 Drakens at present in use by the Swedish Air Force, the first of the more advanced Saab 37 Viggen prototypes flew for the first time on 8 February 1967.

There was a change of wing configuration with this aircraft in an attempt to enhance short take-off and landing (STOL) capability. The delta wing has been retained, but there is also a foreplane fitted with trailing-edge flaps. This combination has proved most effective and the AJ 37 Viggen (129) is able to take off from and land on hard paved surfaces only 1,600 ft (500 m) in length.

One of the most technically complicated aircraft to appear on the aviation scene, with the first flight of a prototype on 14 August 1974, is the Panavia MRCA (Multi-Role Combat Aircraft) **(130)**. Perhaps one of the really remarkable achievements relating to this aircraft was the creation of a design capable of adaptation to meet the requirements of the British RAF, German Air Force and Navy and the Italian Air Force. This was followed by the formation in 1969 of an international company—Panavia—combining the talents of the British Aircraft Corporation, Germany's Messerschmitt-Bölkow-Blohm and Italy's Aeritalia to build this very important 'swing-wing' aircraft.

The technical complication comes from the need to produce an aeroplane with multi-role capability, and much of the structural complexity is associated with the very advanced wing. Conventional flying controls are replaced by a 'fly-by-wire' system, in which triple redundant circuits and electric actuators move the aircraft's control surfaces. Most complex of all is the highly sophisticated avionics system which features terrain-following and attack radar together with a laser rangefinder. It is estimated that more than 800 MRCAs will be built to meet the needs of Germany, Italy and the UK, with the first deliveries going to the Luftwaffe in 1978.

The British defence system has available no early warning and control aircraft such as the Boeing AWACS being

developed for the USAF.

Instead, this country relies upon the NATO radar system, covering the whole of Europe and its approaches, to give RAF interceptors time in which to scramble and investigate any potentially hostile aircraft.

Russian reconnaissance aircraft are frequently busy far above the North Sea, and the illustration (131) shows a Soviet Tu-95, known to NATO as 'Bear-D', being shepherded by a Royal Air Force Phantom.

131

130

Hawker Siddeley Aviation in Britain has developed the only operational fixed-wing vertical/short take-off and landing (V/STOL) strike fighter in the Western world.

Originating from the company's P.1127/Kestrel series of aircraft, the Harrier is in service with the Royal Air Force, the illustration (132) showing typical terrain into which and out of which these aircraft can operate, right up alongside front-line positions.

This capability comes from the remarkable Rolls-Royce Bristol Pegasus vectored-thrust turbofan engine used in the Harrier. With its nozzles rotated vertically downward the aircraft lifts off the ground supported by jet reaction. As height is gained the nozzles are rotated progressively rearward until the aircraft is moving forward fast enough for the wings to generate adequate lift.

Potentially the most important version of the Harrier is that designated AV-8A, a single-seat close-support and tactical reconnaissance aircraft for the United States Marine Corps (USMC).

The first of these was delivered on 26 January 1971, and the total number of firm orders received by early 1974 amounted to 102 aircraft, including 8 TAV-8A two-seat trainers.

Illustrated are five AV-8As (133) of one of the USMCs squadrons which are already operational.

133

132

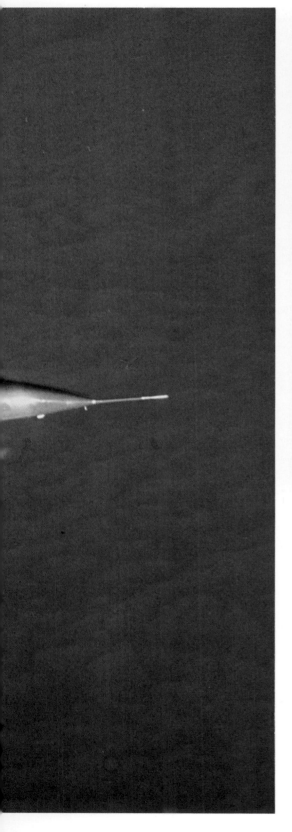

135

The cost of developing complex new aircraft is fast becoming beyond the means of any private company. This has resulted in international collaboration on many projects, both civil and military.

Typical is the Société Européenne de Production de l'Avion (SEPECAT), the Anglo-French company formed by Breguet Aviation and British Aircraft Corporation in 1966 to produce the Jaguar supersonic strike fighter/trainer for the air forces of France and Britain.

To date, four versions are in production: the Jaguar A single-seat strike version and Jaguar E (134) two-seat advanced trainer for the French Armée de l'Air. Corresponding versions for the RAF have the designation Jaguar S and B respectively. The British S differs from its French counterpart by having an advanced inertial navigation and weapon aiming system, which is integrated with an on-board digital computer.

Another international collaboration has produced a new two-seat basic trainer, advanced light strike and battlefield reconnaissance aircraft, the Franco-German Alpha Jet (135) designed and produced jointly by Dassault-Breguet in France and Dornier in Germany.

First flight of a prototype was made on 26 October 1973 and the first production aircraft are scheduled for delivery in 1976.

Manufacture of the outer wing panels, tail unit, rear fuselage and cold-flow exhaust is carried out by Dornier, who are responsible also for final assembly of the close-support version. France builds the rest of the airframe, and assembles the trainer versions. Power plant, common to both, consists of two SNECMA/Turboméca Larzac turbofan engines, each of 2,976 lb static thrust.

13

Impressive in close-up is Fairchild's new single-seat close support aircraft for the USAF, the A-10A **(136)**, selected for production by a fly-off competition held during the latter half of 1972. It features a new 30 mm multi-barrel gun and can carry up to 16,000 lb (7,257 kg) of weapons on external pylons.

It should be appreciated that the maximum loaded weight of this single-seat aircraft is slightly in excess of the maximum loaded weight of a World War II Boeing B-17C Flying Fortress.

Having taken a fairly extensive look at military aircraft, past and present, it seems desirable to conclude with a brief glimpse of the wide range of civil transport aircraft in use today. After all, it must surely be the hope of all mankind that one day we shall become sufficiently enlightened to dispense with military aviation and weapons of war forever.

One of the most successful small feeder-liner transport aircraft designed and built in Britain in post-war years is the Britten-Norman Islander **(137)** which was produced originally at Bembridge in the Isle of Wight.

Following acquisition of the assets of the company by the Fairey Group in 1972, a production line was established at Fairey SA's Gosselies, Belgium, factory, eliminating the production hold ups which had presented many problems to Britten-Norman's management over a long period.

With accommodation for a pilot and nine passengers, the rugged and reliable Islander has found buyers all over the world, and its improvement and production seem likely to continue.

In America the Gates Learjet Corporation builds several aircraft of much the same capacity as the Islander, but which are as different as chalk from cheese.

Learjets are luxury executive aircraft powered by twin turbine engines, and emphasis in the company's latest Models 35 and 36 has been to improve comfort and instal turbofan engines to offer greater economy of operation. The Learjet 35 **(138)** has accommodation for a crew of two and from eight to four passengers according to the standards of luxury required. The range of this version with maximum payload is 1,698 miles (2,732 km).

139

PT-DTY

14

41

This page:

The Netherland's best seller has been the Fokker-VFW F.27 Friendship, a medium-range turboprop-powered airliner which has accommodation for a crew of two and a maximum of 48 passengers in all but the Mk 500 version, which has an optional high-density seating arrangement for 56 passengers. Well over 600 of these aircraft have been sold, and the very colourful example illustrated is a Mk 400/600 in the service of Royal Air Inter **(141)**. Britain also has a successful turboprop airliner in much the same size category, namely the Hawker Siddeley 748, with normal accommodation for 40–58 passengers. Like the Friendship, it is powered by two of the reliable and economical Rolls-Royce Dart

In the largest category of airliners pride of place is taken by the current Queen of the Air, the magnificent Boeing 747 which—whether Boeing like it or not—will be remembered as *the* Jumbo jet.

The first of the world's wide-body large-capacity commercial transports, it heralded a new age of air travel, and on 1 June 1975, almost $5\frac{1}{2}$ years after the 747's introduction into airline service, Boeing could announce that the combined fleet of these aircraft had carried more than 90 million passengers, and that they had flown more than 1,420 million miles (2,286 million km). This picture of a Boeing 747B of South African Airways, ready for take-off on a night flight, depicts the grace—and glamour—of these wonderful aeroplanes **(143)**.

43

Preceding page:

Very similar in appearance to the Learjets is the Falcon 20 **(139)** produced by Dassault-Breguet in France. This has normal accommodation for a crew of two and 8–10 passengers, but it is possible for as many as 14 passengers to be accommodated in reduced-pitch seating and by the elimination of tables.

Britain's equivalent is the Hawker Siddeley HS125, with a crew of two and a maximum of 12 passengers in the Series 400. Hawker Siddeley and Beech Aircraft Corporation had a marketing agreement, with Beech being responsible for the North American sector of the market. In this area the designation of the Series 400 is BH 125-400 **(140)**, that illustrated being operated in Brazil.

turboprop engines which have contributed so much to the success of many other aircraft.

Just the right combination of engine and airframe is, so often, the key to an airliner's popularity with operators and, more importantly, the passengers. A good example is British Aircraft Corporation's One Eleven, its various series powered by two rear-mounted Rolls-Royce Spey turbofan engines. Illustrated is a Series 500 of British Caledonian **(142)**, which accommodates a maximum of 119 passengers. Well over 200 of these aircraft have been sold, and utilization of the type by operators such as Allegheny, Braniff and American Airlines speaks much for the competitive performance it has to offer.

No mention of current civil airliners would be complete without reference to the current Queen of the Air—the magnificent Boeing 747 which—whether Boeing like it or not, will be remembered forever as **the** Jumbo Jet.

The first of the world's wide-body large-capacity commercial transports, it heralded a new age, and on 1 May 1974, just over four years after the 747's introduction into service, Boeing could announce that these aircraft in service had carried more than 63 million passengers, and that they had flown more than 1,001 million miles (1,611 million km).

It seemed logical that a freighter version of the Boeing 747 would appeal to many operators, leading to the 747F. This ground shot of the nose loading door **(144)** gives a good impression of the aircraft's size, particularly when it is pointed out that the height of the nosewheel tyres in the foreground is 4 ft 1 in (1.24 m).

It was a foregone conclusion that, so far as American manufacturers of commercial transport aircraft were concerned, the Boeing Company could not be allowed to have a monopoly of the market for wide-body jet airliners. The first to follow Boeing's lead was the Douglas Aircraft Company, a division of the McDonnell Douglas Corporation, whose three-engine DC-10 Series 10 made its first scheduled passenger flight on 5 August 1971. Illustrated **(145)** is a DC-10 Series 30 before delivery to Union de Transports Aériens (UTA).

Last of the three big wide-body jets into service was Lockheed Aircraft Corporation's L-1011 TriStar, powered by the advanced technology RB.211 turbofan engine developed by Rolls-Royce. First revenue-earning flight of the TriStar **(146)** was made by Eastern Air Lines on 15 April 1972.

144

45

46

123

148

Neither could one approach the conclusion of this history without mention of that other remarkable product of international co-operation, the Anglo-French Concorde supersonic transport aircraft.

So much has been written about Concorde that comment seems almost superfluous. The two pictures (**147** in British Airways insignia and **148** in Air France insignia) must serve to illustrate the graceful lines of this aircraft of tomorrow.

Simultaneous take-offs by Concordes of Air France and British Airways were made on 21 January 1976, marking the beginning of supersonic air travel for ordinary fare paying passengers.

As these words were being written, in early 1976, there was still great uncertainty about operation of Concordes into the American international airports at New York and Washington, although there had been an earlier announcement of a 16-month trial period. Despite this, environmentalists and anti-Concorde groups seemed determined to fight this approval of a trial period by all possible means. Almost simultaneously with the appearance of this news, Air France announced that it had recorded a 66.9 per cent load factor on the first 17 Concorde flights from Paris to Rio de Janeiro and 58.3 per cent on the return flights. These figures must be regarded as highly satisfactory for these pioneering services, for the break-even load factor has been quoted as 55 per cent.

Following page:

One other product of international co-operation deserves richly its place on the last page of this history, in the shape of Airbus Industrie's A-300B2 (**149**) twin-turbofan wide-body short/medium-range commercial transport.

Manufactured by Aérospatiale of France, Deutsche Airbus (Messerschmitt-Bölkow-Blohm and VFW-Fokker) of Germany, Hawker Siddeley Aviation of the UK, Fokker-VFW of the Netherlands and Construcciones Aeronautica SA (CASA) of Spain, our picture (**149**) gives some appreciation of the complexity of the advanced technology wing, designed by Hawker Siddeley, which helps give the Airbus such remarkable take-off and landing performance. Its two General Electric CF6-50C turbofan engines provide economic operation— and their quietness is almost unbelievable. to this day. If they had been able to examine and fly in such aircraft as the Boeing 747, Anglo-French Concorde or A.300 Airbus, they would surely have been convinced that their painstaking work to develop the aeroplane had been more than worthwhile.

Acknowledgments

Pictorial History of Aircraft would not be possible without the superb collection of prints and transparencies which have been assembled for this book by John W. R. and Michael J. H. Taylor. Any which are not acknowledged specifically below come from the collection of the 'Father and Son' Taylor team and I am, as always, most grateful to them for their help with this book, as well as to those people and companies mentioned below.

Aeritalia SpA, Print No. 70; Air BP, 2, 3, 4, 14, 45; Air France, 148; Air Portraits, 31, 42; Beech Aircraft Corporation, 100; Bell Helicopter Company, 114; Benjamin, Lewis, 137; Boeing Company, The, 19, 21, 21A, 27, 28, 32, 33, 34, 35, 36, 43, 46, 54, 56, 80, 81, 125, 144; British Aircraft Corporation, 29, 47, 48, 55, 89, 109, 142; British Airways, 87; Brookes, KJA, 52; Dassault-Breguet Aviation, 86, 87, 92, 134, 135, 139; Douglas Aircraft Company, 20, 37, 57, 59, 73, 74; Downie, Don, 103; Fokker-VFW, 49; Fricke, M, 117; Gates Learjet Corporation, 138; General Dynamics Corporation, 123; Gilbert, James, 6A, 8; Grumman Aerospace Corporation, 120, 121; Handley Page Ltd, 51; Hawker Siddeley Aviation Ltd, 127, 133, 140, 149; Hunt, Leslie, 26, 38, 39, 40; International Civil Aviation Organisation, 101; Levy, Howard, 5, 7, 9, 10, 84, 85, 97, 112, 113; Lockheed Aircraft Corporation, 44, 91, 146; LTV Aerospace Corporation, 76, 77, 78, 79; McDonnell Aircraft Company, 75, 122; McDonough, Kenneth, 15; McDougall, H, 18; Martin Company, Glenn L, 63; Ministry of Defence, 83, 90, 93, 131, 132; Northrop Corporation, 67, 119, 124; Popperfoto, 70–71; Rivett, N B, 12; Rockwell International Corporation, 65, 126; Saab-Scania Aktiebolag, 128, 129; Sissons, K, 16, 50, 95, 141; South African Airways, 143; Taylor, Norman E, 58; Teledyne Ryan Aeronautical, 105, 106, 107; United States Air Force, 82; West, Mick, 17; Westland Helicopters Ltd, 110, 111; Williams, Gordon S, 62, 64, 66, 68.